Praise for *Open Turns*

"In *Open Turns*, Hendrika de Vries shows us the twists and turns a young Dutch migrant girl navigates to find an identity in Australia after surviving the devastation of her native Amsterdam under Nazi occupation. This coming-of-age story will inspire the migrant within each of us seeking home. Supported by loving parents, a strong will, and powerful resilience, DeVries reveals the meaning of destiny. You won't be able to put this book down!"
—Maureen Murdock, author of *The Heroine's Journey: Woman's Quest for Wholeness*

"*Open Turns* is a fascinating coming-of-age story about a young Dutch girl who embarks on a journey into the unknown when her family, traumatized by WWII, immigrates to Australia. With strength and chutzpah, 'Henny' finds her place in the new country, becomes a successful swimmer and grows by fighting her own demons that demand her resilience when success does not come as expected. I loved this book and want to hear the sequel!"
—Radhule Weininger, clinical psychologist, teacher of mindfulness practices, and author of *Heart Medicine*

"In *Open Turns*, Hendrika deVries continues recounting her life story, moving from post-war Holland to her new life in Australia. This beautifully written memoir gives voice to women's struggle to find an identity where their place is dictated by men. What makes deVries's memoir so unique is how she vividly shows us the life of a talented athlete fighting for identity and belonging as an immigrant."
—Elayne Klasson, author of *Love Is a Rebellious Bird* and *The Earthquake Child*

"*Open Turns* asks three essential questions that are both mythic and spiritual: Who am I apart from my talents and dreams? What destiny is calling me to become who I authentically am? What does remembering my past add to the texture of who I have become? Moving between becoming and being Hendrika's coming-of-age adventure into herself and out to the world resonates with all of us who have wondered about our identity, our destiny, and our purpose in life."

—Dennis Patrick Slattery, Distinguished Professor Emeritus and author of *The Fictions in Our Convictions: Essays on Cultural Mythology*

OPEN TURNS

From Dutch Girl to New Australian
a Memoir

Hendrika de Vries

SHE WRITES PRESS

Copyright © 2025 Hendrika de Vries

All rights reserved. No part of this publication may be reproduced, stored in a retrieval system, or transmitted in any form or by any means, electronic, mechanical, photocopying, recording, or otherwise, except for brief quotations in reviews, educational works, or other uses permitted by copyright law.

Published in 2025 by
She Writes Press, an imprint of The Stable Book Group

32 Court Street, Suite 2109
Brooklyn, NY 11201
https://shewritespress.com
Library of Congress Control Number: 2025908965
ISBN: 978-1-64742-950-8
eISBN: 978-1-64742-951-5

Interior Designer: Kiran Spees

Printed in the United States

Names and identifying characteristics have been changed to protect the privacy of certain individuals.

No part of this publication may be used to train generative artificial intelligence (AI) models. The publisher and author reserve all rights related to the use of this content in machine learning.

All company and product names mentioned in this book may be trademarks or registered trademarks of their respective owners. They are used for identification purposes only and do not imply endorsement or affiliation.

For my sister, Laura, who was there,

and

for the women and men who dare to leave behind all that is familiar so their children may have a better future, and for all those who receive them with compassion and kindness.

Contents

Prologue: The Woman I Will Be 1

1 You Don't Belong Here............................3

2 The Land of Tomorrow............................8

3 Chess Lessons 13

4 First Glimpses...................................22

5 New Australians.................................27

6 The Promised Land 37

7 Earth Wizardry 43

8 The Aussie Schoolmaster and
the Dutch Warrior Woman.........................50

9 Making a Home 54

10 Visitations....................................60

11 It's a Church!...................................65

12 Tennis Games 73

13 He Belonged in Ki Ki...........................83

14 The Move to Adelaide 88

15 Mates 94

16 Choice and Responsibility........................98

17	Fame	102
18	A Galaxy of Swimming Stars	107
19	New Loki	111
20	Swim Through Adelaide	115
21	Ocean Swims and Beauty Contests	121
22	Working Girls	126
23	You Asked for It	131
24	The Winter Months	137
25	Changes and Champions	144
26	Female Issues and "Secondhand Goods"	149
27	You Are an Impostor!	154
28	Where Is My Hat?	159
29	A Brave Little Boy	163
30	The Americans	168
31	Serendipity or Destiny?	174
32	My Own Hat	182
33	The Mississippi Steamboat Gambler and His Moll	194
34	A Married Woman	203
35	Destination USA	211

Author's Note

In Greek mythology, Mnemosyne, the goddess of memory, mother of the muses, guides the stories we tell ourselves and how we remember them. And while this book is a nonfiction account of the years I spent in 1950s Australia, where I arrived with my parents as a thirteen-year-old Dutch migrant girl, swam with Olympians, and grew into a married woman and mother, it tells the story the way I remember it, or the way the goddess of memory lives in the flesh and bones of a woman who has had a full, long life.

In the process of writing and remembering, I have allowed myself certain literary liberties to preserve the identity of the men and women who are part of my story and to create a flowing narrative, or a good story. To protect privacy and maintain confidentiality, I have changed names and altered personal details. And with a few notable exceptions, dialogues are not verbatim transcripts but verbal representations that preserve and convey the meaning of the interactions.

However, all sports events, places, and times of encounters that form the spine of my memoir are completely factual. South Australian swim competitions and names of competitive swimmers are recorded and can be found in the sports pages of Adelaide *Advertiser*'s online archives.

I hope you enjoy my story.

Hendrika (Henny) de Vries

Prologue:
The Woman I Will Be
Amsterdam, 1950

"Intentions are like prayers," my mother said. "You send them into the universe, and if you pay attention, they come back as destiny."

When my parents, my sister, and I boarded the Dutch ocean liner MS *Johan van Oldenbarnevelt* to join the tsunami of post-WWII European migrants that took our family from Amsterdam, the city where I was born and had thus far been raised, to an unknown future in Australia, I had already decided on the woman I intended to become.

I would be fierce like my mother. I would be loved as my mother was by my father and respected as she was by the WWII resistance workers who were her friends and contacts. I would be independent and stand up for those who were persecuted or deemed inferior, just as my mother had stood up to the Nazis and hidden a Jewish girl in our home. I would become a swimming champion and work at a newspaper, where I would write stories and marry a handsome newspaperman like the protagonist in the novel my friends from the swim club in Amsterdam had given me as a parting gift.

I did not foresee the serendipitous ways in which 1950s Australia would both challenge and shape my innocent intentions into destiny. I had not yet turned fourteen.

Chapter 1
You Don't Belong Here
Ki Ki, South Australia, 1951

I could see it in the derisive grins and wrinkled-up noses, hear it in their snickering comments.

"You don't belong here."

I stood in front of the dozen or so farm kids seated in tidy rows in the one-room school building, the little girls in the front row maybe just a little older than my nearly five-year-old sister, the older boys at the back not quite at puberty.

Mr. Jackson, their seasoned country schoolmaster, had invited me to tell the class something about myself. He had even congratulated me on my English.

What could I tell them?

That I had lived on the cobblestoned canal streets of Amsterdam, witnessed Nazis dragging people out of their homes and holding a gun to my mother's head because we had hidden a Jewish girl? That I had seen old men die on the street in front of our home? That for a long while, we'd had no food? That I had said goodbye to my dad while he stood behind a barbed wire fence on his way to a prisoner of war camp? That he hadn't come home for two years, and when he finally had, he'd been changed and angry because his Jewish friends, whom I had called uncles and aunts, were all dead?

No, way too sad.

Perhaps I could tell them that in my school in Holland, we had studied Dutch but also had to learn foreign languages like French and English. That we'd visited museums where I had seen famous paintings like Rembrandt's "The Night Watch," and I had belonged to a girls' swim club and won prizes because I was a really fast swimmer.

No, too boastful.

"Why don't you tell us something about your long sea journey on the ship that brought you here?" Mr. Jackson suggested gently.

Yes. I could do that.

Since the day it happened, I had been excited to tell someone about the flying fish we had seen in the Indian Ocean just as we were approaching Australia. All the passengers on our ship had run to the decks to watch them. One minute we saw all those fish swimming in the sea, and then suddenly they rose into the sky like a great flock of birds. There were so many of them that they made a huge shadow on the water.

Perfect.

I nodded.

"Today I want you to welcome Henny," Mr. Jackson instructed the class. "It's her first day here at our school. She is from Holland. As most of you know, that's a long way away. It is on the other side of the world—close to England, where our queen lives. Henny will tell you a little about her journey on the ship that brought her all the way to Australia."

One of the boys in the middle row shouted, "But she's wearing shoes. Why isn't she wearing wooden clogs? People from Holland wear wooden clogs."

"Well, she is from Amsterdam," Mr. Jackson explained patiently.

"It's a big city, where people wear shoes, not clogs." He turned to me and gestured for me to speak.

I took a deep breath and thought of my British teacher at Lyceum, my high school in Holland, who'd reminded us in every class to speak slowly and include facts when communicating in English.

"My name is Henny. I came here with many other Dutch migrants on a huge ship, an ocean liner named *Johan van Oldenbarnevelt*. We sailed from the North Sea through the Mediterranean Sea and down to the Suez Canal, where our ship came so close to the shore that I could see men dressed in white robes in the desert. They were Egyptians, but everyone called them Arabs."

"She speaks funny," a couple of the little girls in the front row whispered, loud enough for me to hear them.

A boy in the back snorted. "What's a Soos canal?"

I ignored them and continued with my story. "But the most exciting thing happened when we reached the Indian Ocean, just before we got to Australia. I was standing on the deck when I saw the most amazing thing . . ."

I slowed my story, wanting to make sure they could share my excitement.

"When, guess what, I saw fish come out of the sea and fly. Hundreds of them."

Uproarious laughter and mocking comments drowned me out. The kids turned to one another.

"That's just stupid."

"Fish don't fly."

"She's making it up."

"She doesn't know English."

I could feel the heat flush into my neck and face and turn my cheeks and forehead a dark beet red.

How dare they laugh at me. These spoiled farm kids who had spent their lives in this awful place of rabbits and sheep and hissing flies that lay live maggots. Two of the boys had even arrived at the school in a horse-driven cart that morning. Who were they to call me stupid?

I didn't belong here. Yes, I was stupid—just stupid to talk about watching fish fly across the ocean like birds to these kids who didn't know anything about the world outside this awful place.

"She can't even speak good English!" one of the boys shouted again.

Mr. Jackson stepped forward. "Now, boys and girls . . ."

"You know nothing about me!" I yelled over him—then I ran out of the little schoolhouse, down the narrow, dusty paths through shrubs that emitted buzzing clouds of flies, past a grove of eucalyptus trees, and across the highway, where on the other side, a row of three attached stone cottages sat on the edge of the railroad track. My sleeveless white blouse clung to my chest in the fierce midsummer heat. Sweat trickled down the small bumps of my developing breasts.

I did not belong here. I would find a way out.

I burst into the middle cottage that was now our home. "I do not belong here," I shouted, "and I am not ever going back to that school!"

"Close the door." My mother, standing at the large woodstove, waved her hands. "You are letting the blowflies in."

I shoved it closed, then plonked down on one of the four wooden chairs that the South Australian Railways had provided. Had we really arrived in this awful place only a week ago?

She handed me a plate with a thick slice of fresh-baked bread, still warm and slathered in butter.

It smelled so . . . good.

"You baked bread in the woodstove?" I was impressed.

"Yes, this old woodstove works fine actually," she said. "I baked a couple of loaves. There's plenty more butter. Real butter. Can you believe it? We will never have to go hungry again, Henny." She said this last part firmly, her words a stern reminder to be grateful and not dare to complain.

Chapter 2
The Land of Tomorrow
Amsterdam, 1950

When we were still living in Amsterdam, my mother's traumatic memories and lingering fear of hunger made her an easy target for the charismatic Aussie salesmen who arrived in the Netherlands to sell the dream of plenty for the Australian government after WWII. Armed with government posters that portrayed Australia as the "Land of Tomorrow," their talks promised unlimited opportunities for young Dutch families who had the will and courage to emigrate.

"Just think, Henny; in Australia, no one ever has to worry about going hungry," she told me after first hearing their pitch, her voice expressing a yearned-for but hard-to-believe wish.

Even though it had been almost five years since she and I had nearly died of starvation in the Hunger Winter—a period when some twenty thousand people had perished of cold and hunger in Amsterdam—my mother still hid jars of peanut butter, pots of jams, cans of milk powder, and bags of flour, rice, and beans in closets and cupboards all over the house. "You never know when there will be another famine," she would say, ignoring my complaints that opening any high kitchen cupboard put me at risk of a concussion from being hit on the head by falling jars and cans of food.

When my dad suggested they attend yet another presentation by one of the smooth-talking Aussies who had flooded Holland, my mom readily agreed.

"We may as well go hear what they have to say," she said. "What do we have to lose?"

They left me to watch my four-year-old sister, Laura (pronounced "Lara" in Dutch), while they and interested friends and neighbors headed to the presentation.

They came home with handfuls of colorful leaflets and amazing stories about this mythical land on the other side of the world, a land of eternal sunshine and wide-open spaces Down Under, where apparently the sky was always blue, the weather always balmy, and the food so plentiful that no one would ever starve.

"And plenty of work and no worries about housing," my dad said. "Apparently, every able man with two hands has the opportunity to own his own land and build a family home."

"There are also cute little koala bears that live in eucalyptus trees," my mom added, which was the only part that sounded interesting to me. She looked at me. "Henny, we do have something important to tell you, but first I'll make us some tea."

The serious tone of my mother's voice made me pay attention. As she walked toward the kitchen, I got up off the floor, where I had been reading my sister one of her favorite stories—about an arrogant bear and a clever white cat—went to sit at the table, and waited.

My dad put teacups on the table; a few minutes later, my mom brought in the steaming blue-and-white teapot.

"Henny," she said once we were all seated, "Daddy and I are thinking that we may want to immigrate to Australia."

"You *what*?"

No, they couldn't be serious.

I knew that two of my dad's war buddies and even a family down the street were planning to emigrate. It seemed like everyone was talking about migrating these days. One of our teachers at Lyceum had even addressed it as a historical global issue. He taught us that postwar healing and recovery had remained slow and challenging in Holland. The Dutch economy struggled with a severe lack of jobs and housing for its growing population. Australia, on the other hand, desperately needed young families to maintain its booming economy. Under a government policy called "populate or perish," it had set out to recruit thousands of young Dutch families to immigrate to Australia.

"But surely not my family," my friends and I had said.

We were doing just fine, weren't we? I stared at my parents. Were they crazy?

"I just won first prize and a gold medal in a 100-meter breaststroke competition this year, and I placed third in the Nationals for junior swimmers," I said. "My coach says I only came third because I'm used to swimming in a 25-meter pool. When I start practicing in a 50-meter pool, she says, I could be the fastest girl swimmer in Holland."

My parents did not say a word. I felt anger explode in my head—or was it alarm?

"How can you do this?" I yelled across the table at them. "You both know how important my swimming is to me. And now you want to take me to some stupid country on the other side of the world?"

"Oh, honey," my dad interrupted calmly. "I know that you are an excellent swimmer, but there are swimming pools in Australia."

"Oh, and how about my school? I have school friends—Carla and Denise and all my other friends at Lyceum. You made me pass all those tests to get into that prestigious school. You said it was because I was smart. But now what? It's no longer important?"

"There is no need to be so dramatic," he said. "I am sure that there are good schools in Australia. You are young. You will make new friends easily enough."

My mom met my gaze and held it. "Remember, we're doing this for the family—for you and for your sister. The housing situation here in Holland is not getting any better. Houses were destroyed during the war. Nothing has been built. There won't be anywhere for you to live in a few years, when you reach the age you want to get married."

"Mom, I am only thirteen!"

It was true that my cousin and her new husband had been forced to move in with my uncle and aunt because of the housing shortage. Many young couples were now living with parents or in tiny sublet rooms. Others were emigrating.

"It sounds like I could possibly find work and housing on a sheep station or at least a large farm. It might be good for all of us to spend a year or so in the bush or the outback," my father said quietly. "Get back to basics, to what's important in life."

If my mother was seduced by the promise of food and abundance, my father responded to the lure of freedom in Australia's wide-open spaces, far away from the horrors he'd witnessed during his incarceration in Germany and his grief for the city he had loved but no longer recognized when he returned. His close friends and business colleagues gone, slaughtered in German concentration camps, his spirit yearned for the vast emptiness of the Australian bush.

"The bush or the outback? Isn't that where all the poisonous snakes and spiders are? And no swimming pools, I'm sure." I shuddered. One of my school friends had shown me pictures of the huge, hairy, poisonous spiders that lived in the Australian outback. Their poison could kill you in one minute, he had told me. And there were no hospitals. What was my father thinking? How could my urban mother who loved beauty agree to that? She didn't even speak English.

"Mom, you know, don't you, that they don't speak Dutch there and you don't speak English. We'll be migrants. They'll hate us!" I pleaded with her.

"We will be welcome there, Henny," my mother said. "Australia needs immigrants."

I heard the resolve in my parents' voices. They were serious.

"You have already made up your minds!" I cried and ran into my bedroom, where I threw myself on the bed face down.

"My parents are making me immigrate to Australia—I will never be a swimming champion!" I lamented to my swim coach the next day.

She embraced me. "Oh, Henny. Yes, your parents told me. We will miss you, but so many people are emigrating. I hear that Australia has excellent swim clubs and they welcome Dutch swimmers, since our swimmers have a reputation for being so fast. Don't worry. I am sure we will hear that you have become a champion down there."

I did not know how to respond. I just looked at her, eyes brimming with tears. Could no one stop my parents?

She smiled. "You will be fine. Just don't ever forget that you are a Dutch girl from Amsterdam. Now go swim your laps."

I dove into the pool.

Chapter 3
Chess Lessons
At Sea, 1950

That year, in December, our little family of four joined the tidal wave of hope that swept up thousands of young Dutch families. We left behind all things familiar—family, friends, culture, and language—and boarded the MS *Johan van Oldenbarnevelt* to set sail for the "Land of Tomorrow."

"I'll never see them again. I'm going to miss them so much," I cried to my parents, who stood behind me on the ship's wide deck. I pressed my body hard against the cold railing, leaning over to wave goodbye with all my might to my friends from the swim club who had come to send me off to my new life.

Holding up the banner of our swim club with the white letters ADZ (for Amsterdamse Dames Zwemclub, or "Amsterdam Ladies Swim Club") against a black-and-red background, they continued to stand in the cold winter sleet and wave even as the ship began to sail from the harbor.

Gradually, the gap between us widened. I squinted my eyes to hold on to their image as they became smaller and smaller, until I saw just dots in the far distance. And then they were gone. A cold winter's rain mingled with the tears that rolled down my face.

I clutched their parting gift, a young adult novel about a Dutch girl who becomes a swimming champion, works at a newspaper, and falls in love with the journalist she will marry. The book, which had been signed by fifteen of my swim mates, would become my oracle in the years that loomed ahead, though I didn't know that yet.

"I'm sure you will see them again one day," my mother reassured me. "And you can write to them."

I nodded. She took my hand, and we turned our backs on the land where I had been born and raised.

Carried along by the throng of men, women, and children slowly wending their way into the ship's cavernous interior, we found ourselves inside the once luxury ocean liner that had now been refitted to transport more than twice the number of its original passengers for the immigrant trade.

"Mom, it's huge," I whispered to her.

"Yes, we'll have to watch Laura," she said, grabbing my little sister by the hand.

We followed my father to our designated deck, where we were given a map of the ship's layout and instructed on sleeping arrangements. To provide maximum passenger capacity, there were separate dorms for male and female passengers.

Emigration, it seemed, was big business.

"I'm not going to like this," my mother said when we discovered that the female dormitory consisted of row upon row of bunk beds crammed close together. "They should have told us. It doesn't feel safe."

"Oh, I think it's safe," a woman standing next to us said. "It's a big ship, and these bunk beds are secure—but it is criminal. They are robbing us. We paid good money for this passage, and they're packing us in like cattle."

But I agreed with my mom. All these bunk beds, all these women and girls packed together in this massive space. Ever since we had almost lost our lives in a mass shooting on the last day of the occupation in Amsterdam, I had not felt safe in crowds.

"Laura and I must sleep in the bottom beds, Henny," my mother said. "You will have to have the top one."

What if the boat started rocking? And I would be sleeping right next to a woman I didn't know for six weeks? No, I did not feel safe.

My mom looked at me and sighed. "Oh well, we'll get through this. We've been through worse."

Four-year-old Laura grabbed my arm. "I'll take the upper bed. I can climb up."

My mom and I both started laughing and hugged her.

"No, we don't want you to roll out," I said. "I can take the upper bed. It will be fun."

But it was not fun at all. That night, I could not sleep. The dormitory space echoed with unfamiliar sounds. Women would not stop talking. I heard a girl crying. Someone was snoring very loudly. Kids were giggling, and I heard their mothers shushing them. I missed the quiet safety of my bedroom at home in Amsterdam, the pretty room I had shared with my sister, where we'd each had our own bed and a new little writing desk had sat next to mine. It had been my dad's gift to me when I passed the entrance examination to Lyceum. We'd had to leave it behind. And the small table and chairs that I had used for my make-believe tea parties during the war when there was no food, the ones Laura had inherited—we'd had to leave those behind, too.

My pillow felt wet from my tears, and I climbed down and crawled into the lower bunk with my little sister.

She draped her small arm over me. "I miss Beertje," she whispered.

I too missed our family dog, who had also had to be left behind because of Australia's strict quarantine laws. So much had been left behind. What were my parents thinking?

"I miss everything," I whispered, "but we have each other."

Holding her small body close, I fell asleep.

"It's only for a few weeks," my dad said when we met up with him the next morning and he saw the dismay on our faces. "The male dormitory isn't much better. They're packing us in, that's for sure."

"It must have been wonderful to make a journey on this ship when it was still a luxury liner," I said to my parents as we admired the old carved wood moldings and the majestic center staircase that joined the different levels.

My mother smiled. "Yes, I can imagine women in ball gowns and men in flamboyant tuxedos or evening jackets descending those stairs. But look at us, more than a thousand of us in our everyday clothes, heads and hearts full of wartime memories and pockets empty, traveling to a land we've never seen before."

"And spending our nights in separate dorms," my dad joked, getting a smile out of my mother. "But hey, at least they are allowing us to eat together. Did you know, Henny, that you only just made it?" He turned to me. "You will be allowed to eat your meals with us adults because you are thirteen years old."

Unfortunately, children twelve years and younger, which meant my little sister, were consigned to separate children's dining rooms and tables. Another decision that upset my mother.

Overwhelmed by the enormity of the ship's size and my awareness of my mother's unhappiness about the sleeping arrangements and her constant worry that Laura, who liked to wander and explore, might fall overboard, I clung to my father's side during the daytime.

"Henny, you should explore the ship's activities," he encouraged me later in the first week on board. "Have you checked out the pool?"

"Yeah, but it's crowded with kids throwing balls and people splashing each other." I scrunched up my face. "And you know, Daddy, the water sloshes like giant waves from one side to the other. You can't really do any serious swimming."

"Why don't you sign up for the chess class, then?" he suggested. "You like playing chess."

I did like playing chess. My parents had played regularly at home and taught me the basic moves. It sounded a lot better than getting in that overcrowded swimming pool.

"That's a good idea, Daddy," I said, nodding. "I'll do it today!"

When I signed up for the chess classes, I was put in a level above the beginners, where I met Pieter, who was around the same age as me. We sat across from each other, and as we reviewed the value of the different chess pieces and practiced simple moves, the instructor praised us and said, "You kids are off to a good start."

"I plan to become a chess master," Pieter said as he showed off his knowledge of chess openings.

I liked the way his curly brown hair flopped over his forehead and right eyebrow when he smiled at me. He was a good chess player, and I enjoyed playing him. He beat me and others in the practice games, but I could see a weakness in his game, and I began to think that I might be able to beat him sometime. Swimming competitively with my girlfriends in Amsterdam had taught me that competition could be fun.

"Always observe your opponents' moves," my dad had taught me.

I did this with Pieter, and I noticed that he sometimes moved his pieces too fast and often sacrificed his queen, or the valuable bishop or knight, unnecessarily.

Still, I liked his confidence, so I was thrilled when he asked after our lesson one day, "Want to go for a walk around the deck?"

On our walk, Pieter told me he had taken chess lessons back in Amsterdam and had definite plans to join a chess club in Sydney.

"You're a good chess player for a girl," he said with a big smile.

I liked his voice, and the fact that he held my hand as we walked, but his comment annoyed me a little. "Girls play as well as boys," I responded, and added with snarky satisfaction, "You didn't need to sacrifice your queen in our last game."

He tossed his hair back, grinned, and said, "I won, didn't I?" Then he added, "If I plan to become a grand chess master, I need to learn to take risks in the game."

He sounded a little boastful, I thought, but I still liked him holding my hand. I also liked that he would wink at me when he practiced with others in our group.

The next day, the ship's first junior chess tournament was announced. Since our games had improved quickly, Pieter and I were both moved to advanced status for the tournament.

"I know I will win," Pieter exclaimed. "No one on this ship can beat me."

I laughed. "What if *I* beat you?"

"Girls are not as good in competitions as men," he joked.

Or maybe I thought he was joking.

"Why won't Pieter talk to me anymore?" I asked my mom plaintively. "Should I have let him win?"

I had felt nervous and unsure of myself on the day of the tournament, despite my dad's encouragement—"You could win in your age group, if you stay focused," he'd said that morning—so I'd been as shocked as Pieter seemed to be when, after a long, hard game, I'd won first place and beat him into second.

After that, he'd abruptly stopped speaking to me; he turned his back every time I tried to approach him. But I refused to believe that my winning had made him not want to be my friend anymore.

"I must have done something horribly wrong," I told my parents.

My parents exchanged a look, and my dad took me aside.

"It's not your fault," he said firmly. "Some boys do not like girls who are smarter than them. But remember, that's their problem. Never make yourself less smart for a boy." Then he grinned and added, "Your mom often beats me at chess, and I like her a lot, don't I?"

I nodded and managed a small smile.

I felt less sad after that conversation with my dad, but it still seemed unfair to me when Pieter started walking around the ship holding the hand of another girl. She didn't even play chess.

We reached the Suez Canal a few days after that. Navigating through the narrow canal, which I had learned about in school, I was amazed at how close our large ship sailed to the shore. I felt that I could almost touch the white, glistening sands of the sun-drenched Egyptian desert.

Men in white robes on small crafts circled our ship and climbed on board to sell their exotic souvenirs. It seemed that almost every passenger on board was charmed by their smiles and effusive sales pitches; people crowded the decks to view, peruse, or buy at least one of their colorful scarves, intricate necklaces, or beautifully carved alabaster animals.

One of the men tried to cajole my mother into buying a necklace. "For a beautiful lady," he said, smiling, but she just laughed. Then he showed us one of his small carved camels. He pointed to me, but I thought it would be perfect for Laura.

"Oh, Mommy, Laura would love that," I said.

But my mother objected with a scowl. "We don't need outrageously expensive trinkets." I had been eyeing one of the colorful necklaces for myself but thought better of it after my mother's comment.

"We should save our money for our new life in Australia," she said, and my dad agreed.

The excitement of that experience was topped only by the thrill of seeing the flying fish in the Indian Ocean a week or so later—but now I would never talk about that again.

The New Year arrived while we were still on the Indian Ocean. I was with the older children who were allowed to stay up with the adults to celebrate the ringing in of 1951 at midnight. We had been practicing for days to sing the popular Scottish "Auld Lang Syne," a song most of us from the non-English-speaking world had never heard of before, and as the clock approached midnight, people gathered in groups, held hands, and began to sing.

When midnight struck with loud banging and cheers, I felt myself caught up in a large swaying, singing, cheering, hugging blob of people. A familiar panic made it hard to breathe, and the noise hurt my ears.

"Mommy." I grabbed my mother's waist with both arms and pressed my face against her chest. My dad reached out from behind her and put his hands on my head.

"You are safe," my mom whispered into my ear. Then, more loudly, "Look at all these people. There are so many of us. In our best migrant clothes, our pockets empty, our hearts full of hope and intention. I pray we did the right thing."

I looked up and saw the tears that filled her soft brown eyes.

My dad said in a loud voice that carried through all the noise and excitement, "We'll be fine, Miep. There'll be plenty of food, work, and sunshine—and no more separate dorms."

My face was once again resting on her breast, but I felt my mother smile.

As families dispersed, the ship echoed with wishes of "Happy New Year!" and "To a New Year—to our new life."

But I suddenly missed my school and swim friends very much. I wished we were back in Amsterdam.

Chapter 4
First Glimpses
Fremantle, Western Australia, 1951

"We can see Australia! Get up, everyone. It's Australia!"
My fellow passengers' shouts of excitement awakened me not many days later. Groggy from sleep, I dressed quickly and accompanied my mom and Laura to the deck, where my dad joined us and it seemed the whole shipload of over a thousand passengers had rushed to gather.

"We can see land! It's Australia! Look, it's Australia!"

"Aren't you just a little bit excited?" my dad asked.

I nodded. "Yes."

"And a little bit curious?" He turned to my mother.

"I'm just hot." She laughed. "You will need to buy me a summer dress."

We had left our old life in Amsterdam in midwinter and were about to start our unknown new life in midsummer Down Under.

We were approaching Fremantle, the port of Perth, Western Australia's capital city, the first of our Australian stops before we would disembark in Sydney after almost six weeks at sea. My parents, my sister, and I held hands as we watched the western coastline of the country that would become our new home come nearer and nearer.

When the ship docked, we were given permission to wander

through the town of Fremantle for the next few hours, with the strict order to be back on the ship by dinnertime.

It felt strange and exciting to put our feet on solid land after all the weeks on the ship.

"We are actually in Australia," I said, laughing with my mom and dad. "Can you believe it?"

"Are you sure this is Australia?" my dad joked. "Where are the kangaroos?"

We laughed with excitement and curiosity as our feet trod the ground of the land we hoped would become home.

I turned to Laura, whose little face looked flushed. "Wow, it's sure hot here, isn't it?" I said.

Clearly not dressed for the extreme Western Australian summer heat, she and I peeled off our cardigans and stripped down to light sleeveless blouses, but my mother huffed and puffed.

"I really do need a summer dress," she said.

"Well," my dad said, chuckling, "let's buy you one."

As we walked by a series of shop windows displaying women's dresses, he pointed to a white knee-length dress with short cap sleeves. The dress was dotted with red and orange tulips.

"How about that one?" he said. "It will remind you of Holland."

"We shouldn't spend money right now," my mom protested, but my dad brushed away her concerns and ushered her into the store.

When she tried it on and showed it to us, I agreed that my dad had excellent taste. "It looks beautiful on you, Mommy."

I had never seen my mom act so young and girlish as she looked coming out of the store wearing her "tulip dress," as it would be named from now on, and I wasn't surprised when my dad said to Laura and me, "Girls, you have the prettiest mother in all of Australia."

His words warmed my heart and only further affirmed my intentions to marry a man who would love me just like my father loved my mother.

Laura and I were getting thirsty, and I had spotted a shop a little farther down the road from which people were exiting with ice creams and strange metal beakers. The marquee read "Milk Bar," and we discovered when we entered the store that the place served large drinks concocted of ice cream, whole milk, and various flavors. The drinks were called "milkshakes" and served in the huge stainless-steel containers in which they were mixed. Since the war, our meals in Amsterdam had consisted of small portions, with dessert only a once-a-week treat and usually just a small cup of vanilla or chocolate pudding. So in the face of these gigantic ice cream–filled beakers, my parents decided one would be big enough for Laura and me to share.

"You choose the flavor, Henny," my dad said.

"How about strawberry?" I suggested, turning to Laura.

She nodded eagerly. "Strawberry sounds good!"

We each had our own straw and took turns slurping away as we sat on a bench in the sun outside the milk bar.

I have never in my life forgotten the delicious sweetness of that very first strawberry milkshake on my tongue.

Our taste buds satisfied, we wandered around under the amazing light of a cloudless blue Australian sky and admired the unique architecture of Fremantle's colonial-era buildings and homes with their lovely verandas. Feeling the warmth on my skin, tasting the sweet strawberry milkshake still lingering on my tongue, and watching my mother's enchantment with Fremantle's Victorian architectural style, I felt an unexpected surge of joy. Yes, I was actually walking on the ground of the promised land of plenty, far, far away from the dark winter skies and wartime memories of armed Nazis with swastika armbands searching the houses of Amsterdam for people they sought to slaughter.

"Look," my mother said to us, "those front verandas with their filigreed wrought iron work are a perfect design for carefree conditions in a warm climate. They are just like the pictures on the recruitment posters the Australian government representatives back in Holland showed us."

As I listened to my mother's enthusiasm, I sensed that she felt reassured. "See," she seemed to be telling herself and us, "we were not lied to. We can be happy here."

My maternal grandfather was an architect and a contractor who had built and designed homes and churches in my mother's native Rotterdam, a city bombed and destroyed by Hitler. My mother had inherited her father's love for beauty and design. When I was a little girl, she'd taken me for walks along the canals of Amsterdam and pointed out the gables and unique shapes of the stately seventeenth-century canal homes. "Always look for the beauty," she'd always said. "There's plenty of ugliness and cruelty in the world, but there is also so much beauty."

On this day in Fremantle, I fell in love with Australia, not yet aware of the challenges ahead. "Let's stay here and not go back to the ship," I said to my father. "It's beautiful here. And I bet there is a swimming pool."

My dad smiled but reminded me, "Henny, we are scheduled to disembark in Sydney, where we must still pass through a customs examination and an immigration indoctrination. We can't just decide to stay here. That's why they kept our passports on the ship. Remember, we are immigrants. We'd better obey the rules."

My thirteen-year-old mind bristled at the rules and regulations my father had just pointed out, and it made me think about our new situation more deeply: In Holland, I had been just another Dutch girl, but here, I was an immigrant, a migrant. What did that say about me? How did that make me different from the girl I'd been in Amsterdam or set me apart from Australian girls? What did it really, really mean to be an immigrant, a migrant?

Chapter 5
New Australians
Bathurst, New South Wales, 1951

"Will we see kangaroos and koalas?" I asked my father excitedly.

"I don't know," he said, "but we will be traveling through the Blue Mountains. I hear they are magical. Better keep your eyes open."

Our long sea journey had finally come to an end on January 21, the day prior, as our ship sailed into Sydney's harbor. After an overnight stay on board, we'd disembarked and passed through a rigorous customs process, and now we were about to board the train that would take us to the migrant reception center in Bathurst, some two-hundred kilometers west-northwest of Sydney, where we would be processed into our life as "New Australians."

I wasn't sure what it meant to be "processed," and I did not, in fact, see any kangaroos on the journey, but my dad was right: The train ride through the Blue Mountains did indeed make me feel like I had landed in a magical place.

Accustomed to the straight horizons of the endlessly flat landscape of the Netherlands, where I had ridden my bicycle on weekends and holidays under dull gray skies, the multihued, mountainous vista that revealed itself through the train windows cast a spell on my thirteen-year-old psyche. My father had passed on to me his love for myths and fairy tales through bedtime stories when I was a little girl. As I watched the awesome mountains reach high up into glittering sunlight and then drop down into steep, hidden valleys of actual dark blues and green, my imagination entered a mythical kingdom, the backdrop against which the adventure of my new life would begin.

Yes, I could live here.

The buses that would take us to the camp were waiting for us when we arrived at the railway station near Bathurst.

Unfortunately, the enthusiasm the majestic beauty of the Blue Mountains had generated in me was quickly squashed as we approached the migrant processing center.

"This is where we are going to live?" I turned to my parents in horror. "It's so ugly!"

Through the bus windows, I stared at row upon row of dilapidated old huts and sheds, some with broken windows, that would apparently be our home.

"This is where they are going to put us!?" my mother exclaimed. "It's not just ugly, it's dirty," she said, her voice sounding angry and tired.

As we climbed off the buses, we were met by clouds of dust and flies.

We learned that the camp had originally been constructed as an army camp and had been hastily thrown together to prepare young Australian men to go fight in WWII. Just two years after the end of the war, it had been transformed into a processing and instruction center for "New Australians," the young European families like ours that the Australian government needed and was actively recruiting to support its economic "populate or perish" recovery plan.

The original army camp had been constructed to house only 1,500 soldiers, but the migrant camp had five times as many inhabitants at a time. Our accommodations consisted of unlined and unheated iron sheds and timber barracks in poor condition, freezing in winter and unbearably hot in summer. Quarters were portioned off for married couples, but the flimsy partitions offered little privacy.

My parents, Laura, and I were housed in a single room. Another family occupied the room on the other side of the thin partition. We could hear everything that was said or done on either side. The overcrowded conditions in the camp felt brutally demeaning and disempowering.

Families ate in communal dining rooms. The food was ample, but the night after our first meal, I woke up to my mother retching and running outside to throw up.

"Are you all right, Mom?" I asked her the next day.

"I'm fine," she said, "probably just something I ate."

But when she continued to throw up after each meal, my dad and I insisted she see the camp medic. She resisted until I got angry with her.

"This is not fair," I scolded her. "You are making Daddy, Laura, and me worry about you. You would make us see the doctor if we were throwing up all the time."

"You're right," she said, her resistance melting. "I'll go today."

My dad took her later that morning, when I was in class, but it turned out the doctor was not very helpful.

"He thinks it's my nerves," my mother said. "Probably anxiety. I told him that I think it's something I'm eating. He didn't want to hear that. Told me the camp food is the best food I will get anywhere. He made it sound like I should be grateful and just stop throwing up."

She sounded frustrated.

Both my dad and I tried to make her feel better.

"Miep," my dad said, "you keep saying that you cannot stand this camp, that it is ugly and dirty, that there are flies everywhere—and we both hate that we have just one room for the four of us. Isn't it possible that your nerves are reacting?"

She shrugged and said stubbornly, "I think it's the food."

"But then why are Daddy, Laura, and I not affected?" I asked her.

"I don't know," she said. "Maybe I have a sensitive stomach."

Even though the frequency of her vomiting decreased over time and stopped almost completely after we left the camp, my dad and I continued to worry for a long time about my mother's "nerves."

Years later, when I revisited the camp—which by then had become a historic site honoring European immigrants' many positive contributions to Australian society—I would learn that digestive upsets were common among the camp immigrants due to the fatty mutton that was served daily to people who had suffered long periods of starvation and were used to light diets. Their digestive systems simply could not handle the fatty foods.

My mom had been right, as she so often was.

We had arrived midsummer, a time when the heat and flies were at their worst, especially the noisy blowflies—so named because instead of buzzing like normal flies, they made a loud, aggressive hissing sound. I learned quickly that they drop their live larvae on any exposed flesh or raw meat.

I watched with fascination one afternoon when I saw blowflies descend on the skinny shoulders of an eight-year-old little Dutch boy whose sunburn blisters had created a nasty open sore on his shoulder. He brushed the flies away but didn't manage to do so before they dropped their maggots, which immediately crawled all over his shoulder, into the wound, and up his neck.

As the boy writhed and screamed, trying to flick away the maggots, my stomach twisted, and I almost threw up right there.

The camp medic, however, laughed at the boy's cries. "Hey, you want to be an Australian? Can't let flies and maggots bother you, mate. Wait till you meet our huge, poisonous spiders and snakes."

"You shouldn't be so mean to that little boy," I wanted to say to the medic, but the maggots had made my skin crawl, and I just wanted to run away. Luckily, by then the boy's cries had attracted several women to comfort him, so I did not feel so bad about failing to stand up for him.

Still, I shuddered. How were we going to live in this country with its disgusting flies and maggots?

"You are here to become New Australians," our lanky, serious young Australian teacher lectured us. "Remember, from now on, English will be your only language. Your goal is to become assimilated into the Australian way of life and culture. You will eat Australian food and study Australian history and civics. You will stand up for the Queen of England and sing the anthem of 'God Save the Queen' to honor her before every class and every movie or community event."

School-age children were expected to attend daily classes in the large school tent. It was made clear from day one that we were being taught to become Australians. It was also made clear that even if we learned the language fluently and assimilated, we would never be "real Australians" but would always be "New Australians." The speech our teacher was currently delivering was one we heard every day.

Lecture done, we stood at attention to sing "God Save the Queen." When we finished singing, I put my hand up. "We have a queen in

Holland also," I said when the teacher gestured for me to speak, "but we don't sing to her."

He stepped toward me, a frown splitting the sweating middle of his forehead, and responded to me by addressing the whole class in an extra-loud voice: "Listen, all of you. Now that you are in Australia, you are subjects of the Queen of England. You must renounce any queen or king you had, or you cannot become an Australian."

Confused, I asked, "Can't I honor two queens? And why does Australia not have its own queen?"

"No, of course you cannot serve two queens," he snarled impatiently, scowling. "If you want to be a real Australian, you will only honor the Queen of England."

He proceeded to deliver a long lecture about the British Empire and the Commonwealth that few of us understood, given our limited English, and still didn't explain to me why Australians wanted God to save the Queen of England but I could not acknowledge the Queen of Holland.

Many years later, I would engage in lively discussions with Aussie friends and family in which we would explore the difficult, unanswered questions that remained alive in my young, inquisitive mind. But at this point in time, I didn't yet have the awareness to ask, "Aren't the real Australians the Aboriginals?"

"Mommy, did you know that I can no longer call Queen Juliana my queen?" I asked my mother later that day.

She looked confused. "What do you mean?"

"The teacher told us we can only honor the Queen of England. We have to renounce our Dutch queen—we must give her up. I don't think we can even ask God to save her. Only the Queen of England."

"Oh, that's such nonsense." My mother frowned. "That's all about allegiance, in case the Dutch and the Australians ever went to war—and that will never happen. We can't give up our affection for Queen Juliana and Wilhelmina. They were our queens, and in some ways always will be." She stopped as if to recall a moment long ago. "Remember," she said, her voice softening, "how we used to listen to Queen Wilhelmina's words of encouragement and inspiration on the radio when she was in exile during the war?"

I knew my mother had a lasting affection for Queen Juliana's mother, Wilhelmina, who had been the reigning monarch during the long, hard years of the occupation.

"Yes," I said, "you and your Resistance friends would listen to her when I was in bed. You listened on that secret radio you had hidden behind the partition in the kitchen cupboard."

"To possess and listen to a radio was punishable by death." My mother sighed.

"But you and your friends from the Resistance did it anyway," I said, smiling proudly.

"Hearing Queen Wilhelmina's encouraging words helped us stay in the fight," she said softly. "Freedom never comes easy." Eyes narrowed, she turned to my dad, who had entered the room during our conversation. "We are being treated as if we are inferior just because we are immigrants. It's not good for our daughters."

"Well, that's because in the eyes of the Australian government, we are inferior," he responded. "Remember, we are New Australians; we're expected to speak English and adapt to the Australian culture, because they believe their culture is superior. We knew that when we decided to immigrate here."

"But they need us to shore up their economy—they literally begged us to move here," my mom said. "We are not beggars. We paid our own way. I want you to get us out of this camp as soon as possible. I don't care where we go. We just need to get out of here."

But my parents and others had already learned that the promises made by the Australian government representatives in Amsterdam had been grossly exaggerated and even misleading. Housing in the urban areas of Australia was almost as scarce and difficult to find as it had been in Amsterdam. Land was expensive, loans difficult to obtain—for immigrants, in any case—and most station owners or farmers in the bush or outback preferred to employ single men over immigrant families with children.

The closest opportunity for my dad's dream to spend time in Australia's wide-open spaces came from the South Australian Railways. The Railways representative who came to the migrant camp in Bathurst to recruit workers painted a glowing image of a job in the ninety-mile so-called "South Australian desert." The work consisted of daily trips on a handcart into the empty mallee scrubland to inspect and maintain the miles of desolate railway tracks.

The image of being outdoors in what the representative colorfully described as "the Australian bush" appealed to my dad's post-traumatic spirit. And the fact that the job also happened to include a home for his wife and two daughters sealed the deal.

A town with a swimming pool and high school existed an hour or so away from what would be our new home, we learned. But without an automobile or bus service, it may as well have been on the moon.

Two days before we were to leave the Bathurst camp, all schoolchildren in the camp were taken to an outdoor swimming pool to escape the oppressive heat. I was thrilled to finally be in a pool again and spent the whole day in the water, practicing the swim strokes that had allowed me to win junior races in Amsterdam.

But the pool in Amsterdam had been indoors. No one thought to warn us that our young, pale Dutch skin was unprepared for the intense Aussie sun.

That night when I started to take off my dress to go to bed, I screamed in pain. "Mommy, Mommy, I can't do it—my dress is stuck! It hurts. It hurts so much!"

Tears rolled down my face at the excruciating pain. The skin on my neck, back, and shoulders had been sunburned so badly that every inch was covered in a solid mass of large blisters.

My mother took one look and said, "Oh my God, you can't go to sleep on that. We need to go see the camp doctor right away. It's an emergency."

Fortunately, the camp had its own hospital, staffed mostly by migrants under the supervision of Australian doctors.

The doctor on call took one look at me and said, "Well, young lady, I can't blame you for crying. You managed to get a nasty second-degree burn. I'll give you something for the pain, and you'd better watch out for our Aussie sun. Sunburns are pretty common here."

I nodded. His kindness made me feel a little better, especially after he asked a nurse to slather my skin with an oil that diminished the stinging pain. He handed my mother a large bottle of it and said, "Don't worry. With care, your daughter will grow a new skin."

An apt metaphor for immigrants needing to adapt to their new environment.

Armed with a huge bottle of the soothing oil and an ample supply of wide rolls of bandages for my shoulders, we boarded a train to South Australia a day later. We were heading for the life in the wide-open spaces my father yearned for.

Our new home would be a tiny rural community (home to some four or five dozen people) called Ki Ki. It pleased my mother when the Railways representative told her that Ki Ki was the Aboriginal name for "food and water."

"Think of it as an oasis," he said, "a stopover for food and water in the midst of the ninety-mile desert."

"I will imagine a lush garden with fruit trees and clear spring wells," my mother said, smiling.

It wasn't until we arrived in Ki Ki that we learned and understood the appropriate meaning of the name the Indigenous people had given the place that would be our home: "grubs and water soakage."

Chapter 6
The Promised Land
Ki Ki, South Australia, 1951

"Look at all the rabbits." I had never seen so many rabbits in all my life. There were thousands hopping along the stretches of land that rolled by outside the train windows, creating a living, moving, furry carpet on both sides of the tracks.

"Yes, it's a bloody plague," said the Railways representative who was to accompany us on the initial stage of the journey. "The government needs to do something about them. They're killing our agriculture."

I had been excited to see kangaroos and wallabies, maybe even emus and koalas, on this almost thirty-hour-long train ride through the continent's vast emptiness. Hopefully more of the Blue Mountains again. But most of what I saw through the train windows were long, boring stretches of dry, barren land populated only by rabbits and sheep.

Where were the beautiful Blue Mountains? Where was my father taking us?

Did he know what he was doing?

Night fell and showed only a vast, empty darkness. The pain meds for my burned shoulders eventually pulled me into a deep sleep. I awakened only when the train had to change tracks in Broken Hill.

After a detour to Adelaide, the train finally deposited us at a tiny, single-platform station in the middle of nothing. We stepped off the car into the relentless midday heat of South Australia's summer.

We had arrived in Ki Ki, our new home.

Another Railways representative, a neatly-dressed man, somewhat older than my father had come up from Adelaide to help us settle into our new life. Taking over from the rep who had accompanied us on the train, he smiled at my mother but addressed only my father—who, fortunately, had a reasonable command of the English language.

"Welcome to Ki Ki," he said, shaking my father's hand. "I'll show you to your house."

The two men talked while my mother, Laura, and I walked behind them down a dry dirt path toward two stone structures that stood on the narrow strip of land that stretched between the railroad tracks and the desert highway.

The first structure—"the house of the stationmaster," the rep said—stood apart. A little farther ahead, a row of three small, attached cottages formed the second building. I did not see another house anywhere.

The Railways rep entered the front gate, which opened to the untended stretch of dirt leading to the middle cottage. He pointed to a small wooden structure on the right-hand side. "There's the outhouse," he told my dad. "The dunny, as it's called around here. You will have to empty it regularly. Watch out for the blowflies."

Even though my mother spoke only Dutch, I could see that she understood what was being said by the horrified look on her face and the tightening of her lips.

He pointed to two large, corrugated iron water tanks ahead of us. "That's your water supply. Be careful how much you use. Remember, you are in Australia. We don't know when it will rain. But two tanks should be plenty for your family."

My dad stopped and translated for my mom. I stopped walking. Mesmerized, I stared at the stone wall of the cottage that faced us.

Why was the front wall of the cottage painted in such an ugly black color? How could the wall be moving?

Suddenly, the surface of the wall broke apart into small black pieces. I gasped. What was happening?

Without warning, the broken bits of the wall buzzed and hissed and swarmed toward us. They were heading for my nose, my ears, my eyes. In a flurried panic, I swatted them away. My mother and I screamed at the same time, "Blowflies!"

Our approach had disturbed the disgusting, fat, hissing things from the cool stone cottage walls in the shadows of the verandas, where they had been sheltering from the heat.

"There are hundreds of them!" I screamed.

"Yes. You'll have to watch out for them." The Railways man waved them away. "Don't let them into your house. Be sure to keep your meats covered. They'll drop their live maggots on them."

Did this country have anything else besides rabbits and disgusting flies?

Swatting away at the flies, we stepped into the cottage that was to be our home. Four rooms laid out in a square, with a small alcove that contained a bathtub. The room we entered held a large woodstove, a cupboard, a small wooden fold-up table, and four wooden chairs. It was clearly the kitchen. To our right lay two rooms that each contained two cots with blankets and a pillow. Apparently, basic bedding was supplied. Ahead of us, a door from the kitchen led into an empty room with an open fireplace. If furnished, this would obviously be the living room. It opened onto a narrow strip of dry earth that led to the railroad track, which ran right behind the cottages. A single kerosene lamp stood on a shelf in each room.

No toilet, no running water, no electricity or gas. No other homes. Blowflies. I looked at my father and mother. Had they gone crazy?

My father grinned. "It will be like camping," he said in Dutch.

My mother looked at him in stony silence, her lips pressed tightly together.

"How's it going?" a booming voice exploded around us as a large man with a wide, toothy smile and a heavy Australian accent walked into the cottage.

"Ah, there you are." The Railways rep turned to my parents. "I want you to meet Mr. Ryan. He is the stationmaster. He and his family live in the house we walked by next to the station. Anything you need, you ask him."

"Call me Dennis," Mr. Ryan said, handing my mother a small bag of loose tea, a bowl of sugar, and a jug of milk. "The wife thought you might need a cuppa after your long journey." He smiled at my mom.

I discovered that the English I had learned at school in Amsterdam helped me understand only a few words of what he said. It also occurred to me that my British teacher, who always told us students that he was teaching us the "correct King's English," might have blamed my lack of comprehension on the way this jovial Australian massacred his vowels. He would not have passed my teacher's test for sure.

My mother fetched a kettle from the few pots and pans that had been provided in the wooden cupboard next to the stove.

"Let me," Mr. Ryan said. Taking it from her hand, he stepped outside to fill the kettle from the nearest of the two water tanks.

My dad and the Railways rep followed him, the rest of us on their heels.

He opened the spigot—and all that came out was a thick yellow ooze.

"Oh, crikey." He looked up at all of us, eyes wide. "That's not good, mate."

A drama of epic proportions followed. A ladder had to be brought from Mr. Ryan's house. Mr. Ryan climbed up and looked in the tank, with all of us looking on.

"It looks like a colony of wasps made this tank home," he reported. "No live wasps, just an old hornets' nest in slime. Sorry, mate, this water is poisoned."

"Let me look." It was my dad's turn to climb up the ladder. He peered down into the tank, brow furrowed. "You are right. Not good. It looks like the tank will need to be totally cleaned out."

"Can't be helped, mate," the stationmaster said.

By this point, they had checked the other tank, which, thankfully, was hornet-free. We at least had one clean tank of water.

"We can get this one cleaned out for you, but you'll have to wait for the rains to fill it up," the well-dressed rep said. He stared down at the ground, away from my dad.

"When will that be?" my dad asked, eyes narrowed.

The two other men glanced at each other, shrugged, then looked up at the sky.

"Who knows," Mr. Ryan said. "Maybe a few months. Better tell your wife and daughters not to take too many baths."

Both men laughed.

"Welcome to Australia, mate."

"The belongings that you shipped from Holland are still stuck in Sydney," the rep added. "There's been a bit of a delay, but they should arrive in a few weeks. Hope you can make do for now." He turned to Mr. Ryan. "I will be back in a few weeks to check on things."

"Don't forget to tell your wife to hang the billycan on the gate in the morning," Mr. Ryan said to my dad. "She'll be seeing an old man with a horse and cart. He'll fill the billy with fresh milk from his cows. Has been doing it for years. Good, fresh milk for your two girls. Better than water."

When my dad translated the message for my mother, she asked, perplexed, "What's a billycan?"

"Little bucket," Mr. Ryan explained after my dad translated my mother's question. "Look in your pots and pans cupboard. You'll see it there. It's got the handle." He laughed.

Then, with a nod at my dad, he and the Railways rep walked away.

We all walked into the cottage in silence. My parents sat down at the wooden table next to the kitchen stove, and my mother looked at my dad.

"One year," she said. "You get one year. If we don't move to the city by then, I am taking the girls and moving back to Holland."

My father nodded. "I promise."

A year? We were going to stay here in this awful place for a whole year? How could my mother agree to that?

That night as I fell asleep on the cot in the bedroom that I shared with my little sister, my nocturnal flights back to Amsterdam began.

Chapter 7
Earth Wizardry
Ki Ki, South Australia, 1951

"You and I need to take a walk." My father looked at me, his jaw set in the stern way that some people attributed to anger but I knew just meant he was trying to solve a mental puzzle.

It had been two weeks since our arrival in Ki Ki. Just a few days since I had stormed out of the schoolhouse after sharing my flying fish story.

"I'll have to talk with your dad," was all my mother had said at the time, but she had not sent me back to the school.

My father had just now come home from work and asked my mother to wait with dinner. She had not argued, which signaled to me that they had already discussed whatever it was he was about to say to me.

"Your mom tells me you are refusing to go back to school," he said as we left our cottage. "You know it's the law in Australia for you to attend school until you are fifteen."

"I am not an Australian, and I'm not going back to that school," I said. "I don't belong there."

I followed him across the highway that separated the part of Ki Ki that held the railway tracks, with its workers' cottages and stationmaster's house, from the other side, with its general store, gas pump, meeting hall, one-room schoolhouse, and neglected tennis courts. The cooling evening air felt soothing on my skin after the intense, dry heat of the day.

We walked side by side in silence down the narrow, dusty paths that wound through the unbearable emptiness of the scrub desert that surrounded us. I wished we were walking along cobblestoned streets in my Amsterdam, where grand, stately homes reflected centuries of human history and young bicyclists would be zooming by. I missed my city.

"Look," my dad finally said. "I know this is hard. There is no swimming pool, and you don't have your school friends. But there are things to learn here that will give you strength in your life. It will build your character for the future."

I shrugged and did not answer. My dad liked to focus on character. "It's the mark of a man," he would often say, ignoring that I was a teenage girl in a foreign land. I couldn't care less about a man's character. I missed my friends, and I was bored, lonely, and angry.

"Your mom says you are having nightmares," he said after a beat, taking a different tack.

"No, I don't think they're nightmares." I shook my head. "I think I am just flying back to Amsterdam because I miss it so much."

He nodded but remained silent. We walked on.

"I flap my arms like a bird," my words spilled out into the silence. "Then I fly across the ocean to Amsterdam. In the distance, I can see the spire of the Western Tower—you know, near our house. I sort of hover across rooftops and look down on familiar places, like the canals where we walked and I rode my bike, but my feet never touch the ground. And I never see any of my friends or any people, but I know they are there having fun."

I stopped to look up at my dad. He remained silent.

"Then I spread my arms again and flap them up and down and fly back. It's dark and a long way back over the ocean. I always wake up in my bed here. And it's weird, but my arms really do feel sore from flying, and I am tired and terribly sad. It's stupid, I know. But it feels so real."

My dad nodded. "Probably is real to your spirit."

We walked a while longer, in silence once again.

When we reached a grove of ghostly gum trees, he pointed at the sloughed-off bark. "See how these trees shed their bark?" He tore off a piece and handed it to me. "If trees lost their bark like this in Holland, they would die. But nature has helped these trees to acclimate to these conditions. They have learned to shed their skin to grow and adapt."

"Why do they have to adapt? Why can't they be the same?" Despite myself, I wanted to hear him explain. My dad had a way of explaining things that made nature seem magical and the universe a grand mystery just begging to be explored, bit by bit, until we discovered its secrets.

"Well, you are smart; you know we can't just act in the same way when we are in a different environment," he said. "You don't wear the same clothes in a winter rainstorm as you do on the beach in the summer."

"Well, yeah, but putting on an overcoat or carrying an umbrella is different from growing a skin that you can shed." I shook my head and pointed at the gum tree. "Besides, that's just a tree. We are people."

"You don't think we are part of nature as much as that tree?" my dad quizzed me, the way he always did when he wanted me to think more deeply about things. "Don't we depend on the air, the water, the nutrients in the earth that grow our food, just as a tree does? We are part of nature, and nature can help us adapt, too."

I frowned. "You think nature is going to help us grow new skins that we can shed? I don't believe that."

"You are right," he responded. "Maybe we need a different kind of adaptation because we are human beings and not trees. But because we are part of nature, we can discover that for ourselves. It is nature's mystery, its magic. Remember, you used to believe in magic."

And then you brought me here to this awful place, I wanted to say, but some part of me felt comforted by the feeling of closeness this conversation was giving me. It reminded me of times back in Amsterdam when he and I had spent precious moments together in our kitchen—temporarily transformed into a photographic darkroom—sorting the negatives of photos he had taken with his tiny 35mm camera, placing them under the enlarger, and watching images emerge like magic on the paper that lay submerged in its alchemical bath.

Ever since I was a little girl, my dad had seemed like an earth wizard to me. Although he did not talk much, I knew his mind sought to escape the limits of our understanding, to go beyond the boundaries and knowledge of our human awareness. But since we'd left Amsterdam, his attention had been on other, more practical things. I had missed our former closeness.

Our mutual walking rhythm slowed down to where it seemed to match the scrubland that surrounded us. I stopped and put my palms on the smooth, white bark of one of the gum trees, standing tall in a sparse grove.

"Yes, feel the tree, really feel it," my dad said. He put his hands on mine against the tree—then, breaking off a eucalyptus leaf that he held under my nose, he added, "Now breathe deeply and smell this."

I breathed in the pungent smell.

"Now close your eyes and listen very carefully." He smiled.

Listen to what—to him, to the tree? Was he trying to tell me that trees talk?

I closed my eyes. I could feel the smooth skin of the tree beneath the palms of my hands as I breathed in the eucalyptus smell. Then, with my eyes tightly closed, I began to slowly hear it. I heard the sound, or the no-sound, of utter, deep stillness—a stillness that crept into my flesh and bones through my palms, my nose, and now my ears. I listened as if the stillness were a foreign language trying to communicate, and I heard the voice of the ancient land. An overwhelming sense of calm slowed my breathing and crept over me.

"Let's go home. It will be dark soon." My father stepped away.

We walked home slowly, the quiet between us broken only now and then by the sound of a scuttling rabbit or other creature. I breathed in the air's eucalyptus scent and noticed that it filled even my mouth with pleasure.

"Koalas eat eucalyptus leaves, you know," my dad said as if reading my thoughts.

"When are we going to see real koala bears?" I asked.

"They are not really bears," he said. "But maybe we should ask one of the farmers around here, what do you think?"

"I don't think they want to know us. We are New Australians." I shrugged.

"Maybe we look and sound strange to them, like this land does to us," he said.

Annoyingly, my dad could always see the other side of things.

"Well, they need to adapt," I said in my best teacherly voice.

We both laughed.

"They will in time," he assured me, "and so will we."

I reached out for his hand. He squeezed mine in response. We walked in silence along the dusty paths through the sparse growth of the mallee shrub and its fragrant, ghostly gums. The land wrapped us in its stillness; the lonely sound of a lost nightbird vanished in the distance.

Without warning, night descended on us.

I was used to the lingering hours and long summer evenings in the Northern Hemisphere. At this latitude, dusk was brief, and without city lights, total darkness swallowed up daylight at an astonishing speed. I held my dad's hand tighter.

"Look up at the sky," he said.

I had never seen stars so bright and in such multitudes. We were standing in the dark stillness under a vast canopy of twinkling lights.

"There are so many of them," I whispered in awe.

"Just think," my dad said, "we are standing beneath millions of universes, and we are all linked together somehow."

He pointed to two particularly bright stars. "See how they point to the constellation of the Southern Cross?"

I could make out the Southern Cross and now recognized it from the stars on the Australian flag.

"The physical universe is always there to guide us," he said, and I heard the reverence in my rational father's voice. This was his church.

In the distance, the tiny light of an oil lamp in the window of our cottage showed us that we were almost home, where my mother and sister would be waiting for us with dinner.

"By the way," my dad's voice boomed through the silent air with loud reassurance, "your mom and I will see Mr. Jackson about you getting high school lessons by correspondence. You will probably have to pass a test in English. We will have to see how we can manage that."

I didn't know what to say. "Thank you, Daddy," would have sounded empty and dumb. But I knew that he understood, as if it were his own, the relief, love, and gratitude that I felt in that moment. This was how he and I so often communicated, not with our words but in a deep, shared silence.

That night, I dreamed a different dream:

I am standing in the middle of a dusty patch of large rocks and dry mallee shrubs, surrounded by tall, ancient eucalyptus trees that are in the process of shedding their bark. It is dusk, and I feel anxious, because I should be flying to Amsterdam. The air is still warm, and I have the uncanny sense that the eucalyptus trees are holding me back and trying to address me. The words are unclear, but a powerful energy emanates from them and holds me in place.

They are talking to me. It is undeniable. I become very, very still.

I know in my bones that I am in the presence of an awesome, timeless power and that its source is the ancient land on which I am now standing. I cannot make out any distinct words. I do not need to. I understand that the land has greeted me. I take my first careful steps . . . and I wake up.

That dream marked the end of my nightly flying-to-Amsterdam excursions.

It would be many years before I would learn about the Australian Aboriginal mythology of "Dreamtime" and the Indigenous shamanic practice of flying in soul-retrieval rituals.

One day in the distant future, while studying depth psychology and immersed in Jungian analysis, I would speak to an analyst who would interpret this dream as a compensatory dream created by the psyche of a young, homesick girl.

But I have always preferred to believe that it was the Australian land itself that spoke to me.

Chapter 8
The Aussie Schoolmaster and the Dutch Warrior Woman
Ki Ki, South Australia, 1951

"We have come to talk about Henny's schooling," my dad said, leaning forward in his seat.

We were seated on the wooden chairs in Mr. Jackson's schoolroom for a meeting requested by my parents. I was thrilled my parents were advocating on my behalf.

"I have already addressed this issue with the representative of the South Australian Railways," my dad said. "When I was hired, I was promised that there was a school here for Henny. I was misinformed, and we need your support."

Mr. Jackson looked puzzled. "We do have a school here. This is the school."

"Yes, but"—my mom interrupted the conversation speaking Dutch; my dad quickly translated her words into English for Mr. Jackson—"when the Australian government representatives came to Amsterdam encouraging families to immigrate to Australia, they promised that all immigrant children would be able to continue their education at the proper level."

"The Railways also said that my job included both housing and schools for my family," my dad added in his own words. "And your school is not at the proper level of education for our daughter."

Mr. Jackson's face flushed. "This is an approved, good school, and Henny can use her time here to improve her English."

My mom interrupted by waving her hands between the two men and again speaking in rapid Dutch.

Mr. Jackson turned to my father with raised eyebrows.

"What my wife said," my father patiently explained, "is that Henny was in her second year at Lyceum, a high school in Holland. Before we left, she was studying French, English, and higher mathematics. Your school is not a high school."

Mr. Jackson nodded but did not speak.

Undaunted by her lack of English, my mother rattled on in Dutch.

"My wife heard on a radio program in Amsterdam that Australia has a long-distance education program with correspondence lessons for children who live in the bush or outback," my dad translated. "And the Australian representatives said that program is also available to any immigrant children who live too far from a school."

"Yes, but she lives right here," Mr. Jackson said, looking perplexed. "This school is not too far."

"But it's not a high school," my dad emphasized. "And we live too far from the high school in the next town for her to attend there, so we think Henny should qualify for correspondence lessons."

Mr. Jackson remained silent for a minute or so, a frown furrowing his forehead. Then, addressing my father directly, enunciating each word with care, he asked, "So you want my support and agreement that my school cannot give your daughter the education level that was promised?"

Realizing that my future was about to be decided, I bit my bottom lip so hard I drew blood. *Oh, please God*, I thought, sending up a silent little prayer, *don't make me go back into that one-room schoolhouse with those awful kids. Please. Please.*

The dear schoolmaster looked at each of my parents and then at me and sighed. "Well, I guess. If that's what you think is best for Henny, I'll see what can be arranged with the correspondence school in Adelaide."

My dad thanked him and stood up to leave, but my mother turned to him and, pointing at Mr. Jackson, said, "Tell him that I want him to teach me English."

"My wife just said that she wants you to give her English lessons." My dad grinned at Mr. Jackson.

The kindly country schoolmaster looked at my mother as if he had just been asked to personally teach the mythical gorgon Medusa, who could turn men to stone with just a glance. He stammered something about not having time, but my mother—the Dutch woman who had survived Nazis holding a gun to her head—would have none of that.

"You teacher. You must teach me. Your job," she said carefully in her best, practiced English. Then, raising her voice to an almost threatening level, she wagged her finger at him. "You will teach me good English."

I could scarcely believe that I was watching my mom wag her finger at the schoolteacher—but this was the mom I remembered from the time when it was just her and me, when she joined the Resistance after Hitler had my dad and other Dutch military personnel shipped off to labor camps in Germany. I had kind of missed that mom.

My dad managed to bring his usual calm to the situation, conveying the Dutch respect for schoolteachers and, of course, that he would pay for my mom's private lessons. An agreement was reached, and everyone shook hands, my mother looking quite satisfied about it all.

I marveled at the ways she manifested her intentions, and as I felt my excitement about correspondence lessons grow, I hoped I had inherited her determination.

I was never quite sure how it was all handled, but two weeks later, I found myself on the train to Adelaide with my mother for an appointment at the South Australia Long Distance Learning School, where, once I passed the English and other tests, I was enrolled in its first-year high school class.

The classwork was taught and monitored by correspondence and included courses in English, French, Latin, Geography, and Math I and II. Each week, a packet of work arrived. It included reading and study assignments, as well as tests that I had to return by mail to be graded and evaluated.

I enjoyed the mental challenge of most of the courses, but especially the creativity required to write short essays in English on the books that accompanied the assignments. The story of *Anne of Green Gables* especially filled an emotional need for me, since her challenge to adapt to new surroundings, combined with her thirst for independence, was an experience with which I strongly identified. I spent hours seated at the kitchen table, writing and rewriting, anticipating with relish the complimentary comments the teachers would send back to me. Their encouraging remarks satisfied my need to have my mind recognized and restored a part of the scholarly identity for which I had been valued in the life we'd left behind in Amsterdam.

Every afternoon, I took a break from my own studies and spent half an hour helping my mother with her assigned English homework. She did not have a natural talent for foreign languages, but her hard work made up for it.

Chapter 9
Making a Home
Ki Ki, South Australia, 1951

"Problems are just challenges to be overcome," my mother proclaimed in her no-nonsense tone of voice that did not permit any expressions of victimhood. And with her usual unyielding determination and energy, she set about making Ki Ki our home and creating a routine for the year that she'd agreed to be there.

First thing each morning, I obediently hung our billycan on the garden gate and watched with interest as a wrinkle-faced old man climbed out of his horse-driven cart and filled it to the brim with fresh milk from one of his large milk cans. Very occasionally, he and I would exchange a friendly "hello" or "good morning," but for the most part, he seemed to prefer an unintrusive wave and a warm smile.

Being my mom's designated translator when my dad was at work, I accompanied her on her daily visits to the small general store on the other side of the highway. Since the train only stopped at our tiny station in one direction once or twice a week and the store was the only grocery outlet for miles around, those of us without automobiles were completely dependent on the grocer for our food supply.

We quickly learned that he did not like immigrants and that he kept strict store hours—closed on weekends and all Christian and Australian holidays. No exceptions, not even for emergencies.

On our first visit, he rolled his eyes and snickered with contempt at my mother's attempt to say eggs, flour, butter, and jam in English when she ordered her groceries.

"Why don't you people learn to speak proper English if you want to live here?" he demanded sharply.

I bristled at this insult, but my mother, seemingly unruffled, just carefully counted out the shillings and pounds that were so different from the Dutch guilders and coins she was used to.

"Hurry up," the grocer snarled.

"You shouldn't speak to my mother like that," I told him in my best high school English.

"Shut your mouth, girl," he snapped, then uttered something that I couldn't quite understand about "dirty Europeans who eat garlic and yogurt, which is just sour milk." The last part, though, I heard clearly: "I will never sell that disgusting stuff in my store."

"What a nasty, rude little man," I said to my mom when we left the store. "You can't let him talk to you like that, Mommy. It's not right."

"No," she said, "it's not right or wise for a shopkeeper to be so rude to his customers, but since his is the only store available to us, he holds the power right now. He clearly does not like migrants"—she grabbed my arm—"but he will have to get used to us, because we are not going away."

Hearing the fierceness in her voice, I was reassured, if still angered by the grocer's disrespect.

"Also, he is right," my mom said with a shrug. "I need to learn to speak English if we are going to belong here."

As soon as we got home, she took out the latest homework Mr. Jackson had given her. She spent the next hour or so bent over the papers at the kitchen table, concentrating on her lessons.

* *

When my mother discovered that the Ryan family's Australian sheepdog had recently given birth to a litter, she marched us over to their home to claim one of the pups, saying, "We need a dog to help us forget Beertje."

We all missed our beloved postwar family mutt, who had been my sister's companion from the time of her birth. Because of Australia's strict quarantine laws, we had been forced to leave him with another family in Amsterdam when we emigrated.

Laura, especially, still grieved his absence.

"They are not Beertje," she said that day, eyeing the black-and-brown puppies tumbling over one another under the watchful eye of their sheepdog mom in the Ryans' living room. But when one climbed aggressively over his pile of siblings to lick her hand and chew on her fingers, she laughed.

"He's tricky," she said, grinning. And she decided that if Beertje was happy in Amsterdam, maybe it was okay for "Tricky" to come home with her.

"He is tricky, but you cannot call him that," Laura told my dad when he came home. "He has to have a proper name."

My dad, who loved mythology, took my little sister on his lap and said, "You know, sheepdogs are clever, and they use trickery to guide the sheep where the farmer wants them to go. So maybe we could name him Loki. Loki was a god of trickery and mischief in the Norse stories that our great-great-grandparents told way before you were born."

She held the puppy, stroked and patted it, and tried it out—"Loki, Loki."

The pup responded by climbing up to lick her face.

"It's a good name," Laura proclaimed, smiling.

Loki it was.

We both learned more about sheepdogs' cleverness or trickery later that year when we were invited to a yearly sheep-shearing event on one of the nearby sheep stations and watched with fascination how the farmer's mature sheepdog managed to coax the sheep across the grate into the shearing area.

Using this as a teaching moment for his daughters, as he frequently did, my dad said, "See how the dog rounds them up until he can trick just one of the sheep across the grate? Then the rest will follow. Be careful," he added. "Don't you ever be one of those sheep that is tricked into just following the others."

I knew what my father meant. Back in Holland, when my parents had sat in our living room with friends and relatives and discussed the postwar question of how it had come about that so many people had blindly followed Hitler in Germany and other countries, my dad had always said that unless people were taught to think for themselves, we tended to be gullible. "Like sheep," he said, "we are too easily manipulated and led along. It's important we teach young people the skill to think things through and not just follow the crowd because it is easy or popular."

Loki soon became part of the family. He cuddled up on the floor or the bed with my sister, responded to the newly learned English words—*sit, wait, good boy*—my mother practiced on him, and made all our daily walks in the monotonous mallee shrub much more interesting. My sister and I loved watching him chase rabbits, of which there were plenty. We could already see how our little sheepdog pup tried to outsmart the rabbits with his bark and cunning. But the clever bunnies were not sheep and always managed to dart away at the last minute, causing him to bark furiously and dash back and forth to us in obvious frustration.

My dad, who had been a skilled marksman in the Dutch military, obtained a hunting rifle and started taking our fast-growing pup along on his hunts for a rabbit or two for our dinner.

"You don't have to come along to hunt them," he told me. "But you should know how to skin them."

But I had no desire to learn how to either kill, skin, or cook rabbits. I left the cooking of all things to my mother. She always impressed me with her culinary skills—skills that enabled her to turn even wild-caught rabbits into a delicious evening meal.

Until one day.

She had left an uncooked rabbit dish to marinate in seasoning on top of the stove before placing it in the oven. A blowfly came buzzing down the chimney and laid its live larvae right on it. Hundreds of gross white maggots were crawling all over the dish within seconds.

The problem of blowflies sneaking down the chimney was solved after my dad put a wire mesh cover on the top of the chimney, but we stopped eating rabbit meat anyway for another sad reason.

On a walk one afternoon, my mother and I observed some rabbits that did not scamper away from Loki. They seemed to be muddled, and they swayed and stumbled as they recoiled from Loki's barks.

"It looks like they are sick," my mother said thoughtfully. "I don't think they are able to see."

In the weeks that followed, we saw more confused bunnies. Some fell over or wobbled when they tried to hop away; others shuffled in zigzagging directions.

"Oh my God, they really are blind. Look! Their eyes are shut!" my mother exclaimed one day.

"It's the myxomatosis," my dad explained.

European rabbits were an invasive species in Australia. Brought over from Britain and released in the late nineteenth century, they lacked natural predators and had taken over the continent. The rabbit population had become a plague that was out of control and so seriously threatening Australia's agriculture that the Australian government had turned to biocontrol. It had released rabbits infected with myxoma—a rabbit-specific virus that caused myxomatosis, a disease that spread rapidly between rabbits and biting insects such as fleas and mosquitos but could not be transmitted to humans.

It did not take long before we began to see hundreds of infected rabbits stumbling about on the paths where we took our walks. Their eyes blinded with swelling and discharge, it would sometimes take them ten days or more to die. Even Loki seemed to take pity on them, and he no longer chased the poor creatures. He would wander over, sniff around, then walk back to us with a look of dejection that we interpreted as grief.

"You are right; there's no sportsmanship in chasing those poor things, is there, boy," my dad would say to Loki.

"I hate this country," I cried out in horror and disgust. "How can they be so cruel!?"

My dad tried to comfort me by explaining the plight of the farmers whose crops and our food sources were being destroyed. But he agreed that "surely there must be a kinder way to kill those poor creatures."

This latest monstrosity was only further proof to me that we should never have come to Australia. What had made my parents think they could make our home here?

I couldn't wait to turn fifteen, when I would be able to make my own life decisions.

Chapter 10
Visitations
Ki Ki, South Australia, 1951

In my quest for independence and what I considered my personal survival, I was trying to figure out my parents. My father clearly enjoyed our life in the emptiness of the mallee desert.

"Daddy," I asked him one morning as he was leaving the house for work, "do you like your work?"

He smiled. "Henny, it's not really work at all. Every day, I step on a little handcart with our young neighbor and I get hours of solitude in nature. Can you keep a secret?"

I nodded.

"It's actually a pleasure." He put his index finger to his lips. "But don't tell anyone." Then he added in a more serious tone, "It's good for a man to be alone in nature sometimes."

There was my dad again, making one of his statements about "a man." I wondered if I would find it a pleasure to spend my day on a handcart in the bush. No, definitely not.

Nature in Australia bore no likeness to the colorful tulip fields and green, grassy meadows dotted with black-and-white cows that surrounded my Amsterdam. Rabbits and blowflies! Where were the koalas and kangaroos we saw on all the brochures?

Ever since we had arrived in Ki Ki, I had been waiting to see a kangaroo up close. All I had seen so far were hopping specks in the distance on the far horizons of the sheep-dotted, stone-covered scrubland farms that surrounded us.

Unexpectedly, I had my first close encounter with a kangaroo that very afternoon, when my mother sent me to the grocery store to buy eggs.

Just outside the grocery store, a large, bloodied kangaroo carcass swarmed by hundreds of hissing blowflies lay on the highway a short distance from our hamlet's only gas pump. It had obviously been hit by a car.

The grocer came out of his store and snarled, "Filthy, stupid animals. They're nothing more than rodents. Now I got to find someone to clean up this mess. That's what you immigrants should be doing."

I had learned not to respond, so I did not say anything, but I was seething inside. Feeling enraged and powerless, I wanted to scream at this man, "You are a disgusting bigot—a miserable, mean, ugly little creepy person!"

Somehow, even just thinking the words made me feel better.

When I got home, I shared the incident with my parents.

My mother shrugged. "Ignore him. He's just an ignorant man."

"Kangaroos are not rodents, they are marsupials," my dad said. "They are shy and tend to be nocturnal. That's why many of them end up being hit by cars and trains at night. Their carcasses need to be removed from the tracks quickly, and the grocer would be pleased to hear that I have already had to clean up a few of those messes. But I have been told that the South Australian Railways often hires Aboriginal men to do the job."

Australian Aboriginals were considered wards of the state. As such, they were not allowed permanent employment—but apparently, they were allowed to do the dirty work no one else wanted to do.

Tears pricked my eyes. "That's just awful. That's as bad as how the Nazis treated the Jews and how the grocer thinks about us migrants."

I did not yet have much awareness of the Australian government's racist attitude toward the Aboriginal people. But my childhood in the heart of Nazi-occupied Amsterdam had made me painfully aware of the cruel side of our human nature. I had witnessed firsthand how easily some of my own country men and women had turned on those they deemed inferior and how frighteningly fast prejudice could morph into brutality and the dehumanization and extermination of people who were considered "other" or "lesser."

My dad looked at me and said thoughtfully, "Yes, unfortunately, we still have a long way to go as human beings."

"I wonder why we always label those who do our dirty work as inferior," my mom said, her voice reflecting the sadness she often expressed at our human capacity to demean and abuse one another.

"It's human nature," my dad said with a shrug. "Hopefully, we are still evolving. It may take a long time."

While his thoughtful response reflected hope, I could hear the fatigue in my dad's voice.

It was not many days later that my dad came home excited from his day's work and told us, "I made a new friend today."

His new friend, he explained, was an Aboriginal man who had been hired to help him deal with the kangaroos and other dead animals that had recently been found in increasingly large numbers on the tracks.

In the days that followed, my dad came home bursting with stories about "dreaming nature" and "mysterious ancestors." One day, he announced with great pride, "Look what my friend gave me today," and showed us a long, narrow shield and spear made of hard wood.

As my mom, Laura, and I inspected the gifts, he said, "Do you know—Aboriginals go on 'walkabout.' They just take off and leave everything behind to spend time alone in nature. It's like a spiritual walk. They follow inner messages their ancestors left them." His voice softened into a hoarseness it often took on when he was expressing an emotion. "I tell you; they know something that we don't know. Something we've forgotten, or maybe we never even learned."

My mom looked worried. "Well, I hope you are not thinking of going walkabout."

My dad took a long puff from his cigarette. "No, don't worry—but I bet many a man after the war would have liked to."

A few days later, he came home and said wistfully, "My friend didn't turn up for work this morning. He left his work shirt and trousers neatly folded next to the track. I am going to miss him."

He would never see his friend again. But he would treasure and hold on to the shield and spear the man had gifted him for years—right up until he passed them on to me.

That evening, I joined my dad when he stepped outside to smoke his cigarette. We walked to the edge of the railway track to look up at the sky in search of the Southern Cross, which we often did. Suddenly, not twenty feet away, a large, shadowy form hopped right up in front of us on the other side of the tracks.

I blinked and stared. "Daddy, look!"

"Shush," my dad whispered, and he put his hand on my arm.

I dared not breathe. A kangaroo so magnificent and huge in size that it made my heart pound stood directly across from us.

My dad and I did not move. I did not dare breathe or utter a word.

The marsupial, taller than my five-foot-eleven father, turned to face us and stood still. We stared at one another. Time stopped as the three of us, father, daughter, and kangaroo, seemed to be held in a timeless connection, an energy field of silent communication where awe mingled with love and respect.

Finally, after what seemed like hours, the splendid creature turned—slowly, very slowly—and hopped away into the night.

"Phew—that felt like a blessing," I said, using words I had often heard come out of my mother's mouth.

"Magnificent," my dad said, his voice hoarse.

We turned and walked back into our railway cottage. Awed by the experience, I found myself overwhelmed by a bewildering mixture of feelings that flip-flopped from hate to fascination to mysterious love for this strange land.

Chapter 11
It's a Church!
Ki Ki, South Australia, 1951

"What on earth...?"

My mother's eyes widened as the roar of automobile engines and human voices on the other side of the railway tracks behind our home pierced the tranquility of our Sunday morning pancake breakfast. Suddenly, the silence of the isolated shrub desert that surrounded us rang with boisterous greetings between men and women and, yes, children's high-pitched laughter.

It had been a quiet morning as we sat around the table reading and feasting on hot pancakes with butter and syrup. The cottage on our right side stood empty, and as always, not a sound came from the cottage on our left, where the gentle man who joined my dad into the mallee for work each day and his shy, young wife preferred to stay indoors and not socialize.

"Hear that? Another car! More people!" my mom exclaimed in disbelief as the voices from across the tracks grew louder and we heard car doors being slammed.

She and I rushed outside to see what was going on. We had noticed the stone building in the grove of eucalyptus trees on the other side of the tracks before, but it had looked abandoned. As we watched now, we saw the engine roar had come from several automobiles, including a shiny 1940s Vauxhall.

Men, women, and children in their Sunday best suits and dresses were climbing out of the cars and greeting one another with laughter and chatter as they walked toward the open door of the hall.

I looked at my mother. "Where did all these people come from?" There were more people here in Ki Ki than the South Australian Railways employees, the teacher, and the grocer? I couldn't believe my eyes.

"It's a church!" my mother exclaimed, surprised. "Why did no one tell us? We're going." She grabbed me and Laura.

"We're not dressed for church," I argued.

"It's a church," my mother said. "God doesn't care. We are clean. Our hair is combed. We are going."

Except for the few times when my mother had taken me to church during the war years, our family had never attended church in Amsterdam. My mother was spiritual, but she'd always depended entirely on her strong inner faith, her powerful intuition, and the dreams she believed were sent directly from God. My father, meanwhile, was an agnostic, a lover of mythology and too much a man of the earth to believe in organized religion or set foot in a church except for weddings and funerals.

Turning to my dad, who had joined us outside, my mother said, "I guess you don't want to go to church with us."

He grinned. "You know I don't, but I will walk over and meet you at the end of the service."

"Yes, I would like that—but Henny and Laura need to come with me," she said.

I wanted to stay home with my dad, and I pleaded with him, "Daddy, do I really have to go?"

"You need to go with your mother," he said. "She needs a translator, and you know I don't go to church."

Of course, I am my mother's translator, I muttered to myself in resignation. *That's my job.* But I did not say it out loud, because I knew it would have made my dad angry.

Holding hands, my sister and I followed our mother across the tracks to join the small group of people who had entered the hall. We sat down quietly in the back pew of the small building, which we now learned was Ki Ki's Congregational Church. The service was in English, but the hymns were mostly familiar to my mother, who had attended the Dutch Reformed Church in Holland with her parents when she was a little girl. The building had a funny, musty smell that made my nose itch. Darn—in the rush, I'd forgotten to bring a handkerchief.

My little sister looked confused and had trouble sitting still. "Why are we here?" she asked me.

"Shush," my mom whispered.

I patted my sister's knee with my left hand and raised my pointing finger to my lips to show her we had to be still.

She squirmed a little, then slumped down in the pew, swinging her legs to show her annoyance. But she perked up during the minister's sermon when he mentioned the word *drop*. His use of the word perhaps had something to do with God dropping goodness on us sinners or our need to drop badness, but I couldn't be sure. I was too busy being mad at my mother for making us do this to pay attention.

"Are we going to get *drop*?" my sister asked excitedly in Dutch.

My mother frowned at how loudly she'd spoken and shushed her again.

Drop was the Dutch word for licorice, which Laura and I had always loved—especially the salty Dutch kind—but which our Ki Ki grocer thought was "disgusting migrant stuff" and refused to sell.

"No, Laura, we are not getting any *drop*," I whispered. "*Drop* is an English word. It does not mean licorice, as it does in Dutch. It means something else."

"What?" she asked with a pout.

I shrugged. "Don't know."

My sister slumped down in the pew again, her legs kicking harder, and I returned to my angry thoughts about our mother, who was happily singing along with the hymns despite her lack of English. She had always had a good singing voice and liked to sing.

My mother was clearly thrilled to be there, and I felt a little guilty that my bad mood would not allow me to be happy for her.

When we left the building with the other congregants at the end of the service, the minister approached my mother with a welcoming smile. A tall young man with curly, strawberry blond hair and twinkling blue eyes, he grabbed both her hands and held them. Way too long, I thought. I could see my mother melt under his gaze, and it made me happy that at that moment, my dad approached the church to walk us back across the tracks.

After being introduced to the minister, my dad lingered to chat with the other churchgoers. His calm, easy manner and gift for storytelling had always attracted both men and women alike. Despite a heavy guttural Dutch accent, he could converse in English with relative ease. When he learned the people present were the owners of the sheep farms that surrounded us, he showed his genuine appreciation for the land.

"Farming is hard work," he said. He asked about the quality of the soil, the lack of water, and their animals, especially the horses.

"You know something about horses?" one of the farmers asked.

"Yes," my dad responded. "I served in the Dutch cavalry at the beginning of the war. Our lives depended on our relationship with our horse."

"I enjoyed meeting your wife and daughters," the minister, who was about to take his leave, interrupted the conversation. "Can we persuade you to join them next time?"

My dad smiled. "No, honestly, you are going to have to give me a pass on that one. I appreciate the spiritual home you provide and that you welcome my family, but nature is my cathedral."

The minister smiled. "We'll keep trying," he said before walking to his car.

"I think nature is as good a church as any," said one of the farmers, a jovial man somewhere in his late forties or early fifties. "And we welcome your little family to our community."

The attractive blond woman at his side whispered something in his ear. He turned and said, "My wife says we should invite you and your wife and girls over for supper next Sunday. She's the boss. How about it?"

My dad turned to my mom, who nodded yes.

And so it happened that we found ourselves at our first dinner in an Australian country home the following weekend, and on our way to becoming part of the community.

Before long, we were welcomed to teas and dinners at the homes of other landowners and their families. We learned from the stories they shared that most had been children of hardworking farmers with little education. They had been expected to help on the farm from an early age. Their relative wealth was only a recent phenomenon, largely a result of the world's increased demand for wool since WWII.

One of the farmers' wives, an especially warm and friendly young woman named Edna, invited my mother to be part of the Australian Country Women's Association, the largest advocacy group for Australian country women and their families.

As my mother's translator, I joined her for her first CWA social and bake sale in the Ki Ki Hall on the other side of the highway. Long tables covered in white tablecloths and laden with platters of cakes, cookies, and pies of every shape, size, filling, and flavor filled the building. I had never seen so many desserts and baked goods in all my fourteen years, and the delicious smell made my mouth water. I wanted to taste them all.

I turned to my mother. "How can those few farm women bake all this?"

"And who is going to eat it all?" she whispered. "There's way too much."

We soon discovered that the South Australian country diet in the 1950s depended heavily on large intakes of sugar and baked goods—a contrast to the lean way of eating to which we had been accustomed in postwar Amsterdam, where our meals had consisted mainly of vegetables, fish, and small portions of meat and potatoes, with a custard dessert as a once-a-week treat and pastries only on special occasions.

Here in Ki Ki, fresh fruit and vegetables were scarce, and our meals now centered on the homemade breads and desserts my mother had learned to bake in her woodstove. I especially liked the Australian lamingtons: squares of sponge cake coated in an outer layer of chocolate and rolled in desiccated coconut.

Despite the hardships, the summer blowflies, and the lack of electricity, telephone, running water, extended family, and culture, my parents became more relaxed that year. My dad no longer showed the angry outbursts that had plagued him after the war and before we left Amsterdam. The painful memories of the war years, which had tested my parents each in their own way, seemed to recede into the past. I could hear it in the sounds of their voices as they joked with each other.

I was relieved to see them in such better spirits. It made me feel happy to witness the calmness that had settled on my dad and the secure, loving relationship he and my mom now so clearly enjoyed.

But a troubling thought interrupted my happiness: Might their contentedness mean they were thinking of settling here permanently?

No, surely, they wouldn't do that to me.

But I worried, especially when they spotted a frame for a double bed in one of the farmers' sheds and made a bid for it. As they threw out the single cots that had come with the sparse furniture supplied by South Australian Railways and replaced them with a double bed, they hugged and smiled in a way that made even the crusty old landowner in whose shed my dad had noticed the bed frame take note.

He turned to me and chuckled. "You are a lucky girl. Your parents really enjoy each other."

He gave my dad an Australian digger's slouch hat as a gift. My father wore it with a swagger as he grinned at my mother and whistled a song off-tune.

My mother laughed girlishly. "Your dad never could carry a tune."

"He seems happy," I said.

"Yes, the outdoor life suits him." My mother looked away.

"I am not staying here," I warned.

"Of course not," she said, sounding surprised. "We are city people, and you are a swimmer. We need to get you back in the pool."

But her words did not reassure me. Hadn't they taken me away from everything I loved once before? I had already been a competitive swimmer then. How could I be sure that they might not find a good "adult" reason to decide Ki Ki would be our future home—especially since they were happy here?

While my mother and father made friends, I spent most of my time reading about young women growing into adulthood. The stories of *Anne of Green Gables* and *Little Women*, mailed to me by my correspondence school, gave me images of heroines I yearned to emulate. I also read and reread, as if it were a Delphic oracle, the Dutch young adult novel my friends from the swim club in Amsterdam had given me as a parting gift.

There were no girls my age in Ki Ki. I missed my girlfriends in Amsterdam. I had turned fourteen, was gaining weight, and felt lonely and restless. My inner heroine swore she would return to Amsterdam to visit all her friends as soon as she could be independent and earn her own money.

Chapter 12
Tennis Games
Ki Ki, South Australia, 1951

"Henny is getting fat. It's unhealthy. I am worried about her."

I was lying on my bed, reading, when I overheard my mother express her concern to my dad, who was drinking an after-work beer in the kitchen.

How dare she call me fat.

I stood up and yelled at her, "Well, what do you expect!?"

My disciplined mother, a lifelong athlete who had been a running and speed walking champion in her younger days in Holland and never gained an ounce of fat in her life, turned and looked at me in surprise.

"I thought you were outside," she said.

"No," I said, "your daughter, who is turning into an unhealthy, ugly, fat blimp with pimples, is right here."

"What—"

"How dare you call me fat?" I hissed. "Remember, it was you who took me away from my swimming, my bike riding. *You* brought me here, where there is nothing to do but eat cakes and more cakes."

"Henny." My mother kept her voice level. "I just want to make sure you'll be fit and healthy to start swimming again when we move to Adelaide."

"Oh, sure." I threw up my hands. "When we move! When we move! If I ever get back in a pool, I will probably sink."

I ran out of the house, slamming the door behind me, and started to walk aimlessly along the railroad track, wishing I could just keep walking, jump on a train, and leave my parents behind.

Soon, darkness began to fall. No train appeared on the tracks, which became more difficult to see by the minute, and I felt the stillness of the night surround and press in on me.

I should have brought Loki along.

Finally, tired and miserable, I turned around and walked back to the cottages.

My parents had started dinner by the time I got back. My mother put a plate on the table for me.

"Of course, you didn't care I was out there in the dark by myself," I whined.

"I knew you'd be home soon," my mom said in a calm voice.

"We are going to have neighbors," my dad announced, as if I had never been away. "An Italian family is moving into the empty cottage next door. The man will be helping me out on the tracks. Dennis Ryan tells me they have two children."

I refused to show my interest. But I wondered if there would finally be a girl my age to relate to.

"I believe they're both boys," my dad added. "One may be close to your age, Henny."

Disappointed, I finished eating my dinner and retired to my bedroom in sullen silence.

As I was expected to, I joined my parents the next day to greet the new family who had just moved in. When we knocked on their door, the father, Mr. Romano, let us in, shook hands with my dad, and invited us to sit on the wooden fold-up chairs provided by the South Australian Railways. The cottage was an exact replica of ours, down to the sparse furniture.

My mother had brought a cake she had baked, and as she cut it into slices, Mrs. Romano set out plates and cups for the fresh pot of coffee she had brewed, which smelled delicious.

As my parents thanked her, she smiled, and Mr. Romano explained in English enhanced by a delightful Italian accent, "My wife does not speak English, but my oldest son, Giorgio, speaks it a little. He learned it in school."

He introduced us to Giorgio and his little brother, Eduardo. We said hello to one another, and I noticed that Giorgio had a nice smile and dark, wavy hair. He looked to be about my age, while Eduardo seemed a few years older than my sister.

Giorgio stood quietly near his mother while our fathers chatted. He was taller than I was and had strong shoulders like a swimmer. I wondered if we could become friends—but we did not get beyond those initial hellos at that first meeting.

In the days that followed, I saw Giorgio only from afar, usually when he was taking his mother to the general store across the highway in the afternoon. One day, he smiled and waved to me. I waved back. I liked his smile.

We repeated that awkward exchange a few times and even managed to voice another verbal hello over the fence that separated our yards in the coming week. Eventually, our shy hellos grew into brief conversations.

One day, Giorgio asked if I attended school.

I told him I was taking high school lessons by correspondence.

His English was more limited than mine, but he managed to convey that he was sixteen and didn't need to go to school.

That was when my dad hit on a plan.

An interesting feature of Ki Ki was its old, neglected tennis courts. At one point in time, it had hosted a thriving tennis club for the surrounding rural properties, as it would again one day in the distant future. The club had been neglected in the postwar years, however, and its weathered court surface showed cracks and small holes through which weeds sprouted. An old net lay twisted on the ground between its posts.

"I think you and Giorgio should play tennis," my dad said to me. "You need the exercise, and he is stuck at home with his mother all day. That's not good for a boy his age."

I was aghast. "No. Daddy, no. I am a swimmer, not a tennis player. I don't even know how to play tennis—and have you seen the condition of those courts? I can't believe that you would even suggest that."

Undaunted, my father approached one of the farmers he and my mother had befriended that week and turned up one day with a bag of tennis balls and two old but still usable tennis rackets. He then approached Giorgio's father. The two men agreed that it was a good idea. Even if we didn't know how to play tennis, we could at least hit a ball or two.

"It will give the youngsters something to do," the fathers said.

"It's a stupid idea," I complained to my mother.

"You will enjoy the exercise," she admonished me. "At least give it a try and then decide."

On the following Saturday afternoon, Mr. Romano and my dad told Giorgio and me to accompany them on the old Ki Ki tennis courts. As they handed us each a tennis racket and a ball, Giorgio and I rolled our eyes, shrugged, and started laughing.

"I cannot play tennis," he said.

"I cannot either," I said. Pointing at our fathers, I added, "And they don't know how to play either, so no one can teach us."

We looked at our fathers and each other and, shrieking with laughter, we shouted in broken Italian/Dutch English, "Nobody here knows how to play tennis!"

"Daddy," I addressed my father, "there is not even a net over which to hit the balls."

He grinned. "It doesn't matter. As you said, you don't know how to play real tennis anyway! But I'll fix it." He set about getting the net back to some semblance of at least a lopsided divider.

Giorgio seemed to like the idea of hitting some balls back and forth over the net, and so that afternoon, he and I began to "play tennis" on the old Ki Ki court. A part of me thought it was stupid, but another part had to admit that I enjoyed the physical activity of running around on the court.

And I did think Giorgio was very good-looking.

From then on, each day when my correspondence lessons were finished, I picked up my racket and called over the fence, "Giorgio, time for the tennis!"

Tennis racket in hand and a big smile on his face, he yelled back, "*Sì*, pronto—ready."

Then we walked across the highway and started to hit the ball to each other.

As the days passed, we got better at hitting the ball back and forth over that lopsided net, and we became more playful.

"Hey, Giorgio, you need lessons," I teased him one day, laughing, when he missed the simplest of hits.

"Oh, you make me so *triste*, so sad," he responded with a mocking crying sound.

The weather had gotten warmer and sweat dripped down our necks and backs. We swatted away flies but kept playing.

One of the farmers, whose house my parents and I had visited, stopped by and shook his head. "You kids need better rackets." He walked onto the court and handed each of us an almost brand-new tennis racket. "They're not new, but they're better than you've got."

As he walked away, he added, "My sister is a tennis player. She is visiting us and will stop by tomorrow and give you some lessons. You need to learn how to serve and do a backhand. You'll enjoy your game more."

After thanking him, Giorgio and I looked at each other and started cheering, "Yes, *sì, sì*, hurrah, finally, somebody knows how to play tennis! Somebody who can teach us!"

After an hour or so of hitting balls, Giorgio walked me back across the highway to the gate of our cottage—the same gate where my mother hung the billycan. We lingered for a while, practicing English words and phrases.

"Say 'billy,'" I teased him.

He responded with a mocking Italian pronunciation of "beelee" until we both hiccupped with laughter. Our attempts at conversation were frequently even less successful than our attempts at playing real tennis, but we were having fun. We also managed to convey to one another that we did not like being migrants.

"I am an Italian, not a migrant," Giorgio said proudly. "I want to show you Rome."

"I want to show you Amsterdam," I said.

I tried to describe my life of swimming, ice-skating, and bicycle riding in Amsterdam. In turn, I was only too happy to attempt to understand what he told me about his home in Italy, where he had friends his own age. With hand gestures, laughs, words, and grimaces, we witnessed and recollected parts of the Italian boy and Dutch girl who had been left behind in Europe when our parents brought us to Australia. In the sharing, we brought them home to ourselves.

It was on that old tennis court that I first discovered how much Australians loved sports and the people who played them. Embracing a sport entitled you almost to the mythical status of being "a true Aussie." Occasionally, sheep or barley farmers from miles away stopped by just to cheer us on, shake their heads, or laugh at "those crazy kids."

One afternoon, an older, bearded man wearing the typical Aussie slouch hat pulled up in a rusty, dust-covered truck. A bottle of beer in his hand, he got out and walked over to our court.

"Hey," he said gruffly, "you kids—you are playing on my court."

We stopped hitting the ball and turned to him.

"We can play here; these are public courts," I said defiantly. "Who are you?"

He laughed, looked at Giorgio, and said, "You have a feisty girl here!"

Giorgio just smiled as I felt my face turn red.

"I'm Jack," the man said. "I heard about you kids giving these old courts some new life. I know you're Australian Newies, but that makes the two of you true Aussies in my book."

I guess we must have looked perplexed, because he laughed. "You must know we Aussies love our sports. Can't be an Aussie if you don't love sport." He walked back to his truck, grabbed another bottle of beer, and returned.

"You kids want a beer?"

We shook our heads.

"You know why they're my courts?" he asked. "I used to play on these courts when we still had a tennis club. Before the bloody war. Well, good on ya, kids." He turned to walk away. "And don't let that feisty girl beat you!" he called over his shoulder to Giorgio.

He climbed into his truck, still chuckling, and drove off. Giorgio and I shook our heads and went back to hitting balls.

I sadly never found out who this Jack really was, but his message stayed strangely imprinted on my mind: *I can be a true Aussie if I love sports—and I'm a swimmer, aren't I?*

"Henny," my mother said to me in a stern voice one afternoon after I came off the court hot and sweaty, "it is time for you to start wearing a bra."

The tone of her voice and concerned look on her face made me feel I had committed some horrible wrongdoing by not binding up my bouncy breasts. I remembered how Giorgio had told me recently that his mother wanted him to marry "a nice Catholic Italian girl." It had not escaped either of our notice that while our fathers were amused by our arrangements, our protective mothers did not allow us any opportunity to be alone with one another off the court.

"I'll make you one right now," my mother said.

Since we did not own a car and did not live near a store where I could try on and buy a bra, my mother, always a whiz with the needle, fashioned me one out of one of her old bras.

When I put it on, I screamed at her, "It gives me pointy breasts that stick out! I'm not going anywhere wearing this thing!"

How could I face Giorgio looking like this? I refused to leave the house for days.

"Giorgio keeps asking me when you can come and play tennis," my father told me on my third day of acting like a spoiled child. "It's not fair to him to just stay away. If you don't want to play tennis with him anymore, you need to go and tell him."

"Fine," I said, and I left the house and walked across the highway to the court, where Giorgio was waiting for me.

I nodded hello and hit a ball but immediately saw his eyes fix onto my pointy breasts instead of the ball. "Stop it!" I screamed at him, then hurled down my racket and ran off the court.

Giorgio ran after me. I was about to unlock the gate to our yard when he grabbed my hand.

I jerked away. "Leave me alone. I hate that stupid game. I hate this place, and our mothers. Just go away . . . leave me alone!"

Giorgio held my hand with a strong grasp and looked at me with such dark, sad eyes that I thought I might fall right into them and never come up for air again. I tried to steady myself on the gate. The pressure of his hand felt protective, not threatening, and I felt my face flush as I held my breath.

He whispered something in his best English that sounded to me like, "Do not be angry . . . I love you . . . you are beautiful."

I could not breathe. I could not think. My stomach had lurched into my throat; my face was burning. His intense eyes locked onto mine and pulled me into a deep, hidden well of emotions I had never felt before. I wanted him to put his arms around me. I wanted to put my face up to his. But all I could do was be still, aware of the warmth of his strong hand on mine and the soft yielding of my rigid body.

"Giorgio!" his mother called over the fence, and mine, right on cue, stepped out of our door.

The spell broke, but our friendship had changed.

In the next few weeks of that early summer, Giorgio and I spent a lot more time hitting balls on that dilapidated tennis court. When the Australian heat became too intense or we had tired ourselves out, we sat on a rock at the side of the court and in halting English phrases shared our dreams for the future.

"Of course, we are going back to Holland and Italy," we told each other. He still wanted to show me Rome, and I still wanted to show him Amsterdam. But I also told him that I liked being able to see the Southern Cross in the sky and that the farmers were nice. He had not met any, he said, and his mother missed her Catholic church and would not attend the little Protestant one. I wanted to show him the Southern Cross but was sure our old-world mothers would not allow us to be alone at night.

Sometimes he held my hand and told me I was beautiful when we walked across the highway back to our cottages. My face always grew hot and flushed at his words.

But the year my mother had promised my father was nearing its end.

Chapter 13
He Belonged in Ki Ki
Ki Ki, South Australia, 1951

I was lying on my bed pondering my parents' control over my future. The midday weather had been too uncomfortably hot for any strenuous outdoor activity the past two weeks, so Giorgio and I played our tennis games later in the afternoon.

One of the farmers had even warned us a few days earlier, "Be careful, you kids; this heat can land you in the hospital." I'd laughed it off then, but after learning later that one of his brothers had almost died of heat stroke, I felt bad that I had not taken his advice more seriously.

"You could always still thank him and apologize," my dad said.

I planned to take his advice but never quite managed to follow up on it.

But it wasn't the heat I was thinking about now; right now, I was busy wondering about my parents' plans in the coming months. Were they as ready to move to Adelaide as they pretended? What about the friendships they had created with our neighbors? And the outdoor life my dad so enjoyed?

"I have no desire to move back to Holland," he had told my mother.

So they were exploring options, and my dad had been checking out suitable work in Adelaide.

When he'd learned the craft of silvering and mirror making after joining his brother in their small glass and mirror business in postwar Amsterdam, my dad had developed a silvering mixture that improved the quality of nonglare mirrors. He called it his "recipe." It had never been patented, and a glass company in Adelaide was now offering him a job with an agreement to buy the famous "recipe."

He had also been advised of a possible office job opening with South Australian Railways, but I knew he wouldn't follow up on that. Recently, I'd heard him say to my mother, "Miep, I will die of boredom sitting in an office all day. If I can't be outside, I need to at least be making something with my own hands."

Could we find a place to live in Adelaide? Rentals were expensive and scarce in the city, especially for migrant families, but loan options to buy a small or rundown house that my dad could expand or remodel were more readily available. One of the Ki Ki farmers had even offered him a personal loan.

"Have you seen Loki?" My sister burst into the bedroom and stopped my wandering thoughts. "I've been looking for him everywhere."

"No." I had not seen Loki for hours. "It's so hot, Laura. He's probably hiding in a cool place."

"I can't find him anywhere," she cried. "I have called and called."

Now just as worried as she was, I followed her into the kitchen. "Loki is missing," I informed our mother. "We can't find him."

She looked up from her Australian Country Women's Association recipe book. "Come to think of it, I haven't noticed him all day either," she said, a frown creasing her forehead.

"We need to go look for him outside," I said. "I'll ask Giorgio if he will come with me."

"Yes, it's way too hot out there," my mom agreed. "And it's not like Loki to stay away for this long."

Eager to help, Giorgio joined us in our search. We walked the paths that led into the scrubland and farms behind the school and the general store. The intense heat, even this late in the afternoon, prickled our skins, and we imagined Loki might be sleeping in the shade of a mallee bush under one of the eucalyptus trees—but no matter how often we all called "Loki, Loki, Loki!" in loud, frantic voices, our lovable, longhaired sheepdog did not jump out or come running.

Sweet Loki, my dad's walking and rabbit hunting buddy, my little sister's playmate, and my mom's target for practicing English commands, had simply disappeared.

We still had not found him by the time my father came home from his day's trek in the mallee desert.

As soon as he arrived, Laura ran to him. "Daddy, Loki is gone. You must help us find him." She grabbed his shirt, tears choking her voice.

"Maybe he has gone for a long walk and is resting somewhere," my mom said, but she did not sound convinced.

"I'm sure he'll come home soon—he's just gone walkabout," I said, reassuring myself and my sister.

"Loki is a smart dog. Probably hiding somewhere from this bloody heat," my dad said, wiping the sweat off his face with his handkerchief. "At least it's cool in here."

"No, Daddy. We looked everywhere, and he is not here." Laura pulled on my dad's hand. "You must go look for him."

He patted her on the head. "I'll go find him. Just let me cool off for a bit." I could hear the fatigue in his concerned voice.

"He is here!" my mother shouted, her voice loud with relief and excitement. She pointed to the bundle of black-and-brown fur pushing at the billycan gate, where Loki usually crawled under the fence to get in and out of the long backyard.

She ran outside and reached him before any of us did. "Where have you been, you wanderer?" she demanded as she reached down to stroke him. "We're sure glad you are back."

But something was wrong. His chest heaving, his head turned toward her, Loki tried to stand but instead collapsed at her feet.

She patted his head and stroked his back. "Oh no, no." She turned toward us and held up her sticky, bloodied hand.

We all crouched down around him. Blood-drenched holes pitted the black-and-brown fur all over his beautiful body.

My dad examined him gently. "Well, my boy. You are not in good shape. Who did this to you, huh?"

Loki put his head in my dad's hand and whimpered.

"He is in pain," my mother whispered.

"Yes, looks like he has been shot with a shotgun." My dad shook his head. "Not good. His body is riddled with buckshot." He turned back to Loki. "Looks like you crawled a good many miles, my friend, just so you could die at home with us, huh?"

"He is going to get better, isn't he?" Laura cried.

My dad put his arm around her. "No, my girl, and you must be very brave, because Loki was very brave. He was in a lot of pain, but he crawled home a long way so he could say goodbye to us. You know, I think he knew he was going to die when he was shot, but he wanted to be with us and not alone. Now we must be very brave, just like him, and say goodbye to him."

Tears streaming down our faces, my mom, my sister, and I huddled around our sweet blood-covered friend, stroking and patting him. For a moment, I felt an all-too-familiar panic clutch my stomach. A childhood memory of other shootings and bloodied bodies in Nazi-occupied Amsterdam surfaced and made the room spin.

Then Laura curled up against me. Survival had taught me early on that you cannot let human cruelty possess you or it will drag you into a dark, helpless hole. Comforting her as she sobbed, I held my sister so tightly I could feel her heartbeat, and the room steadied itself around me.

After a while, my father, with tears in his eyes, said, "It's time. He has suffered enough." With great care, he lifted Loki in his arms, whispering, his voice hoarse, "Come on, boy."

With our sweet dog's blood draining onto his shirt, my dad held him against his chest and carried him away from the house, where he relieved his suffering with a single clean shot from his rifle. We buried his body in the grove of eucalyptus trees where he'd liked to chase rabbits.

We never discovered who had shot Loki. Had he been chasing a farmer's sheep?

"Could've been one of the younger boys," a couple of farmers said. "Maybe thought he was a rabbit."

But no one ever admitted to seeing or hearing anything.

My mother believed Loki's death signaled the end of our time in Ki Ki. "It is an omen," she said. "It's time to move on with our lives."

"Yes," my dad agreed, "he belonged here in Ki Ki."

Chapter 14
The Move to Adelaide
Ki Ki and Adelaide, South Australia, 1951–52

My shock and grief over Loki's painful death drew me closer to my family.

In the days that followed, my parents focused on our move to Adelaide and Laura. Loki had been her playmate and had filled the hole that had been opened in her heart when she'd had to leave Beertje behind in Amsterdam.

In a big-sisterly attempt to make her feel better, I kept saying, "I promise I will get you another Loki," holding her close. I don't think it helped her grief, but it helped me take the focus off my own. Why was there so much cruelty in the world?

Even Giorgio couldn't help. He had not known Loki the way we had.

"He was like an animal angel," I told him.

But he didn't understand and just wanted to hold my hand.

The following week, we boarded the train to Adelaide to inspect the house my parents thought to buy.

My face fell when we stepped inside. The house was even smaller than I had anticipated.

Disappointed, I confronted my father. "Daddy, it has only one bedroom. Where are Laura and I going to sleep?"

"Henny, it's an unfinished house—the plans and permits for an extra bedroom are already in place," he assured me. "I can lay the foundation and build that room in no time at all." He pointed to a small storage room and added, "With a coat of fresh paint, that little space is big and airy enough to be turned into a small temporary bedroom for you and your sister. I can even add a small window."

"It's a cubbyhole," I moaned.

"It will be like—"

"Yes, like camping, I know," I interrupted him. "That's what you said about Ki Ki, and we were there a year, Daddy."

He laughed. "No, I promise—I can get this done quickly."

We walked outside, where fruit trees and a vegetable garden planted by the former owner surrounded the property.

"Look, isn't this lovely?" my dad asked, turning to us all.

My mother smiled. "So now you plan to be a gardener as well as a builder?"

"Why not? It will be fun," he said, laughing.

But I noticed that my mother had been unusually quiet. "What do you think, Mom?" I asked her.

"What I am thinking is that we will own our own home," she responded, expressing her satisfaction as well as approval.

Before returning to Ki Ki to discuss our move and pack up our belongings, my parents took me to the swimming pool at the Adelaide City Baths, where they had made an appointment for me to meet Mr. Major, the coach of the local Chrysler Swim Club. A friendly man with a big, welcoming smile who was known for seeking out and recruiting promising Dutch migrant swimmers when they arrived in Australia, Mr. Major had reached out to my father months earlier, hoping to recruit me.

Greeting us now at the far end of the outdoor Olympic-size swimming pool, Mr. Major told my parents with pride that there were a couple of other Dutch swimmers in his club. "Potential Olympians," he said, beaming. He then invited me to demonstrate my swimming ability.

I dove into the pool. Shocked to find the water much colder than I'd expected, I felt my body respond with an unfamiliar, heavy sluggishness. Yuck—a year had passed since I had swum in the indoor pool in Amsterdam. A year since I had been a skinny, preadolescent junior swimming star, before my breasts had started to grow and I'd gotten fat in Ki Ki, as my mother had said.

I swam slowly. It took my body a while to adapt to the chill. But before I had reached the end of the pool, I recognized the return of a familiar strength in my legs. I touched the wall and tucked in my knees to make the open turn for another lap, and as my feet pushed off with a powerful thrust that propelled me through the water with ease, a strange thing happened. I began to feel a sense of belonging. Not a belonging in either Holland or Australia, but a belonging in my own body. I had forgotten how much I loved the sensation of the cool—or even cold—silky water against my bare skin. I traversed the pool from one end to the next and back again with a smooth breaststroke, and I experienced the sensual exhilaration of rediscovering my own physical strength and aliveness.

"Your stroke is good," the coach said with an approving smile after watching me swim. "With discipline and practice, I think you can be a state champion breaststroke swimmer. Maybe start practicing the butterfly, too. You will have to work hard, though, and we do need to look at your diet."

He introduced me to a couple of swimmers who had just finished their lap training.

"We're aiming for the 1956 Olympics," one of them said after we greeted one another.

"Yes," the other said, laughing. "Join us. We need a breaststroker on our team."

Their goal-oriented enthusiasm triggered memories of the competitive camaraderie that had been such an important part of my life in Amsterdam. A swimmer surrounded by swimmers.

This was where I belonged.

When I told Giorgio the next day that we were moving to Adelaide, he said, "You want to marry an Australian."

The ferocity in his voice surprised me, and I responded with anger, "I am fourteen years old. I don't want to marry anyone. I want to be a swimming champion."

In the weeks we had left, we played our tennis games a few more times. He held my hand, and we attempted to talk about our futures.

"Do you still want to go back to Amsterdam?" he asked me.

"Yes, of course," I said. "One day. But right now I must focus on our move to Adelaide. I am already signed up with a swim club."

"My parents are thinking of moving to Adelaide also," he said, "but I still plan to go back to Italy."

"Maybe we will both end up liking Adelaide," I said, trying to be lighthearted. "We can see each other there. You can always move back to Italy later."

His eyes downcast, he said softly, "I am not sure if I want to live in Adelaide."

"We can write to each other," I said.

A couple of weeks later, when Giorgio and I said our last goodbye, he held both my hands and looked deep into my eyes. "I will miss you," he whispered.

We still didn't kiss, but he embraced me with those deep, soulful brown eyes that made me feel like I was drowning.

"I will miss you too," I said, and I wondered why life always seemed to serve up challenges that demanded we make choices that have no easy answers.

Long after I had left Ki Ki, Giorgio and I met one more time—we ran into each other by chance in the Adelaide Railway Station. He was even more handsome than I had remembered, and his big, dark eyes lit up with affection when he recognized me.

We fell into a comfortable conversation in English, sharing that we were both living in Adelaide, working and "seeing someone."

"Australian?" he asked.

"Of course," I said.

We laughed.

But then he grabbed my hand and said, "You never wrote to me. I loved you."

A flash of heat started in my groin and snaked its way up through my torso to a boiling point in my telltale, blushing face. I felt myself slip into an old emotional confusion. For a moment, we were once again a newly arrived migrant boy and girl navigating the uncharted territory between the old world and the new.

I too quickly dismissed his comments with a light, "Remember what your mother told you: You are a good Catholic Italian boy, and I am a wicked Protestant girl from Amsterdam."

My breezy response firmly reestablished the boundary that kept him in the past, where I felt he belonged. My WWII childhood and experience with postwar migration had taught me that survival demanded the past be left behind. The future was what mattered.

But he didn't let me off the hook so easily; his grip on my hand intensified, his eyes held mine, and with a quizzical, seductive smile, he asked, "Do we still believe that?"

My heart skipped a beat in a moment's pleasure at the pressure of his warm hands and the potency of his gaze. I managed a barely audible "maybe" and let him hold my hand a few moments longer, the two of us standing in merged silence as I tried to still my breath.

Then, he let go. We wished each other the best, and we parted ways. We glanced over our shoulders a couple of times, smiled, then walked resolutely in opposite directions into our Australian lives.

Chapter 15
Mates
Adelaide, South Australia, 1952

Except for a few minor glitches, our move from Ki Ki to the city of Adelaide went quickly and smoothly. Since we were now in the middle of summer and the city pool would close for the winter months, the coach of the Chrysler Swim Club encouraged my parents to have me start serious swimming training right away. Within a couple of weeks, I had joined other members of the club in regular training sessions and was registered for upcoming competitive events.

Competitive swimming in South Australia in the early 1950s gave me an intimate glimpse into the unique Aussie concept of being "mates." In Amsterdam, my swim events had been held in covered indoor swimming pools. In South Australia, competitions were held in open-air pools, rivers, lakes, ports, and the ocean—in short, anywhere there was water.

On many a weekend, members of our club climbed onto a bus or bunched up in individual cars for country carnival destinations in small South Australian towns separated by miles of long, dusty roads. We traveled, all expenses paid, to competitive swim events held in ports and on rivers in towns like Strathalbyn, Port Adelaide, Murray Bridge, and Renmark. It was on these trips that I learned to become an Aussie.

While swimming in the waters of Port Adelaide, I admired aloud the pretty rainbow colors of the water's surface, only to evoke raucous laughter from the boys.

"That 'pretty sheen' we were swimming through was an oil slick, mate," one of them informed me. "But no worries. It can't hurt you."

That was nothing compared to a competition in the Murray River, where I nearly got disqualified from my 55-yard breaststroke event when a water snake slithered around my leg and I almost jumped out of the water screaming, "There's a snake on my body!"

The officials and my teammates just roared with laughter.

I won the race, but I still lashed out at them when I climbed out of the river. "It could have been poisonous and bitten me," I yelled. "It's no laughing matter."

They shook their heads. "Crikey, you are a swimmer. This is Australia, mate. It's not a crocodile. Don't make such a fuss."

I learned quickly that my young friends enjoyed the myth of their Aussie toughness.

"Henny, we're all descended from convicts," one of the boys joked with me one day. "Convicts trying to escape."

"That's why we are so fast, mate," another said, laughing.

"Does being a migrant count as being a convict?" I asked.

"Sure, you're a pretty sheila, and we convicts need our sheilas," one of the louder boys joked as the girls rolled their eyes.

"If you can catch us," I shot back. "Remember, we're fast."

Whether on the road or in the water, we were "mates." Like rivaling siblings, we laughed, we teased, and we took care of one another in our own ways. When one of the girls my age suddenly got her period, cramped over, and could not swim and a young male teammate kept urging her on, an older swimmer scolded him, "Hey, mate, leave her alone. It's her time of the month." He then took the younger boy aside and apparently gave him some much-needed teenage sex education.

I learned about Australian camaraderie and sportsmanship on these trips away. So long as I could tolerate some humorous prodding and was able to laugh at myself, I discovered, I could belong.

"That's the ugliest prize on the planet," my teammates ribbed me, laughing, as we headed back to Adelaide in the bus one day.

When I had swum in Amsterdam, winners of sports events, even eleven- or twelve-year-olds, earned an inscribed medal. I had won a couple of small ones myself. But in the early-1950s South Australian country swimming carnivals, prizes were often donated by local stores that supported the small swim clubs with gifts from their merchandise. Instead of medals or sports trophies, winners of swim competitions were given a decorative vase, a crystal dish, or a ceramic figurine.

On this day, as a prize for one of the events I'd won, I'd been given a ceramic donkey with flowers painted around its neck. About five by seven inches in size, glazed in bright orange and green colors, it was the most garish sculpture I had ever seen.

My swimming mates appraised it as if it were my pet, smirking.

"I love my donkey," I said.

"It's kind of lovable in a hideous way," they agreed with a laugh. "If you like donkeys."

That donkey stayed in my possession for decades, through many geographical moves. For me, it served as a talisman and sweet reminder of the magic of those early innocent days—and the importance of that Aussie "mateship."

To be a swimming champion demanded that we spend every spare moment of the summer months in the pool. We did not have goggles, and most swimmers did not wear bathing caps. Itching, burning eyes and green hair from chlorine were commonplace. But we were young and full of hope and energy, and we all trained hard.

That year, the butterfly swim was established as a designated competitive stroke. With hours of practice, an experienced breaststroke kick, and my developing upper-body strength, I soon mastered it and started winning major breaststroke and butterfly swim events. I would become a state champion in both.

But I was still an immigrant and a working man's daughter. There were other issues to be addressed.

Chapter 16
Choice and Responsibility
Adelaide, South Australia, 1952

By now, my dad had established himself in a well-paying job he liked and was saving money to buy a car so he could drive to work instead of pedaling back and forth, as he had been, on my mom's bicycle that had been shipped from Amsterdam. My mom had found a Congregational Church where she liked the minister and was beginning to make friends, and Laura was enrolled in a nearby elementary school. My dad, Laura, and I had begun to communicate in English at home, though my mom still insisted that she and I speak Dutch. We were adapting.

"We must get you enrolled in the local high school soon," my father announced one day. "I think you and your mom need to go buy your uniform."

"A uniform? I am not wearing a uniform." I looked at my dad in horror.

"It's mandatory," he said.

"Then I can't go to that high school," I argued. "No one's going to put me in a high school uniform. I hate uniforms. Nazis put their children in uniforms."

The thought of entering the local high school as a second-year student terrified me. All the other students would already have known one another for a whole year, and I told myself they would all be comfortable in their similar backgrounds, each with an established friend group. The mandated uniforms only further signaled to me that individual differences would not be considered an asset or even tolerated at this school.

I turned my pleading eyes on my father.

"I won't belong!" I cried. "They'll think I'm weird. They'll all have gone through the first year together, and I'll have to tell them that I was born in Holland, and the teacher will make me talk about being a migrant and the war and why we came here to become New Australians."

My dad regarded me in silence.

"Please, Daddy, don't make me," I begged. "They won't believe I was already in the second year of Lyceum in Amsterdam and that I had to redo my first year by correspondence in Ki Ki. Our life is just too peculiar."

"Well, what do you want to do then?" he asked.

"I want to work and earn my own money. Be independent."

"You realize," he said, "if you already want to be grown-up, you take on all the responsibilities of being an adult?"

"What do you mean?"

"If you're earning your own money, you'll need to contribute to the family financially. You'll be expected to contribute to the mortgage payment, because you are getting room and board here; you'll need to buy some of your own personal things; and I would hope that you would save a little of your earnings each week to put in a bank account, too."

"But I won't be able to earn that much," I protested.

"No," he agreed, "that's why education is important. You want to go to work without an education? What do you think you are going to do? You'd better learn a skill first. If you were a boy, I'd tell you to go to trade school, become an expert at a specific trade."

"I want to work at a newspaper," I declared.

"Well, I believe most journalists in Australia are men, but you . . ." He hesitated.

"Yes, I know—I can learn shorthand and typing because I am just a girl," I finished my dad's sentence with a pout. "I can go to business college."

"You realize business college costs money? High school is free." My mom looked concerned as she entered the conversation, addressing me in Dutch.

I turned to her. "If you make me put on a uniform and force me to go back to school and talk about our horrible time in the war and the hunger and why we came here again, I will go back to Holland. I'm almost fifteen, when I can legally work and get my own passport."

She sighed. "I think you will still need our consent, Henny. Your dad and I will have to talk it over."

I jumped up from my chair. "Sure, you and Daddy discuss your problem daughter. But remember that I work as your translator. Maybe that can pay for business college."

Immediately regretting my words, I snapped my mouth shut.

My mom and I just seemed to annoy each other of late. She treated me like I was still a child, telling me again and again how brave I had been during the traumatic months that she and I had been alone during the Hunger Winter in Amsterdam. She just did not realize or want to accept that I was no longer that little girl, the little girl she loved and remembered and still seemed to want me to be.

How could she continue to treat me like a child when I had to be her translator and constant companion? Why couldn't she let me grow up? Why did she keep bringing up the war? It was in the past. Hadn't I been raised to focus on the future?

"Don't you speak to your mother that way," my father said, his face and voice conveying his anger with me. "You apologize to her right now."

"I'm sorry, Mommy." I turned to my mother. "I didn't mean what I said."

As always, she just smiled and said, "I understand; it's difficult."

I didn't believe she really understood, but after several more family discussions that stressed adult responsibility for my choice, both my parents agreed that I could attend Muirden Business College. I would take the standard courses in Pitman shorthand and typing and earn a certificate in telephone procedure.

Chapter 17
Fame
Adelaide, South Australia, 1953

On a sunny Australian morning, fame snuck into my life. Now fifteen years old, I was fresh out of business school and recently employed in the steno pool of the offices of a local steel import and distributing company. Our office consisted of six teenage girls—two stenographers, two invoice typists, and two file clerks. We worked under the careful eye of the twenty-five-year-old office manager, Brenda, who was also the boss's personal secretary.

I had just taken down a couple of dictated letters and was about to begin transcribing my pages of Pitman shorthand characters when Brenda walked into the steno pool office and said, "Henny, put your work down for a moment and come with me."

What had I done wrong?

Worried, I followed her down the hall and across the truckers' loading area to the main office.

My English was now fluent enough to take dictation in shorthand and transcribe it into a comprehensible letter that pleased the bosses. However, I still had a little trouble making sense of the sexual jokes and innuendos aimed at us by the truck drivers we had to pass to get to the main office as they loaded and unloaded their trucks.

The other girls in the office had alerted me early on to their unrelenting interest in our young bosoms. "Watch out," they'd warned, "the truckers like to make comments about our bodies—especially our breasts."

Mine were by now well-developed and verbally likened to "melons" and "grapefruit" by the guys who leered at them, drew bulbous shapes in the air with their hands, and made disgusting sucking sounds. Initially, their comments had inevitably caused my face and neck to flush a bright purple red—a sign of my discomfort that only seemed to intensify the men's amused attention. But one day, I'd noticed that one of the older drivers, a man with a craggy face and kind eyes that reminded me a little of my father's, reprimanded the younger guys to stop when they gestured, whistled, or made lewd comments. They did not always listen to him, but his quiet support reminded me of what my parents had taught me as a younger child in Amsterdam: *Ignore the bullies and the jerks if you can't beat them, and search out the good people for strength and support.*

In time, I'd learned to simply shrug, mouth the word "stupid" to my verbal tormentors, and turn my back on them. When I did this, the older driver smiled at me and nodded approval, which gave me an odd sense of empowerment and protection.

On this morning, however, the loading area was empty, and my mind was preoccupied. Why was Brenda summoning me? Had I made some horrible mistake?

I followed her to the inner office, where the owner of the company met us. An older Australian gentleman for whom England remained "home" and whose British school education, with its clear enunciation of vowels, made taking his dictation a breeze, he greeted me with a grandfatherly smile.

"Well, young lady, it seems you are a bit of a celebrity."

He led me to the exit door of the main office building, where, on the sidewalk outside, a couple of young men, one of them holding a gigantic camera emblazoned with the words *The News*, were waiting. Reporters? Why would reporters be looking for me?

As soon as they caught sight of me, they lunged at me.

The younger one, who was holding a notebook that looked like one of my own steno pads, stuck a microphone in my face and asked, "How does it feel to have broken two state swim records held by an Olympic swimmer?"

Before I could answer, the one with the camera called out, "Smile—yes, good, look this way. Let's see a big victory smile. Okay! That's a good girl!"

Still confused, I smiled obediently at the camera.

"Will you be training for the next Olympics, and will you swim for Australia or Holland?"

Olympics? Australia? Holland? The questions came way too fast.

I knew that I had swum well in my two butterfly races the night before, but I had not been aware that I had broken Australian Olympic champion Denise Norton's till-now-undisputed state records in both events.

For a fleeting moment, I experienced the dangerous exhilaration of fame and celebrity. My office mates gathered around with interest. I was still the same fifteen-year-old girl, the same young migrant stenographer at the office of a steel company, that I had been a little while ago, but suddenly I had become someone different in the eyes that looked at me.

I learned in that moment that fame, even if brief, had its own agenda, was an independent force that claimed me as its public property and transformed me in the minds of those who photographed and questioned me, wrote and speculated about me, and befriended or envied me.

Who was I in their eyes?

In the following days, neighbors who had never spoken to us before but who had seen my picture in the newspaper contacted my parents with congratulations and even invitations to their homes. People I barely knew suddenly wanted to be my best friend.

I also received plenty of warnings to "not let it go to my head" and invasions into my private life when suddenly my friendship and crush on a blond champion swimmer from Sydney became an object for scrutiny and gossip. It even elicited a snide comment from one of the more prominent mothers of a girl swimmer in our club—"Who does this New Australian think she is?"

I questioned myself in the days and weeks that followed when people who did not know me claimed to have access to my inner thoughts and aspirations.

The dissonance of the experience was dizzying. Yesterday, I'd been a young immigrant girl struggling to learn the language and understand the sexual jokes tossed at me by Aussie truck drivers. Today, I was the "Young Swimmer with a Future," as the caption under the photo in the newspaper stated. I was the Dutch migrant girl who had broken an Australian Olympic swimmer's record.

Australians wanted to claim me as their own, while uncles and cousins in Holland contacted me to make sure I remembered that I was Dutch. "Of course, you will swim for the Netherlands," they wrote me, "when," not "if," I swam in the next Olympics.

One evening as I struggled with the fault line within me, I asked my parents, who were seated in our living room reading the newspaper,

"If I make it to the Olympics, should I swim for Holland or for Australia?"

My dad looked up, surprised. "Henny, the next Olympics are not for another three years. I wouldn't start worrying about that now if I were you."

My mother agreed. "A lot can happen between now and then."

I would learn soon enough that destiny has her own capricious way of unfurling the path ahead.

Chapter 18
A Galaxy of Swimming Stars
Adelaide, South Australia, 1953

"What makes you love to swim so much that you are willing to spend hours each day training for events like the one tomorrow?"

Just before the young reporter asked me this question, I had been practicing for a medley swim demonstration event to be held the next evening in our Adelaide City Pool, where a group of us would demonstrate our proficiency in all four swim strokes.

I had to think before answering. I never felt happier than when I was swimming, but I had not reflected deeply on why that was so until this moment.

Could I share that I became a different person in the water? That in the water there was no fault line—no Dutch me, no New Australian me. No flashbacks to the sound of Nazis kicking in the back door of our home in Amsterdam. No fear or confusion. Just focus and calm. A feeling of safety.

No, too personal.

I could share that I loved the competition. Sort of true, but not completely, because I also loved to swim alone. The feel of just the water and me, in the flow.

No, too complicated.

"Swimming makes me feel strong," I said. "It's fun."

The reporter grinned.

Right answer.

Have you ever had a time in your life when everything just went your way and you naively thought it would always be like that? I was sixteen years old and on top of the world. A year had gone by since I'd broken Olympic swimmer Denise Norton's 55-yard butterfly records, and life bustled with excitement and change. My parents had bought a brand-new house closer to my mother's church. My dad now owned a car and drove me to my swim practice each morning on his way to work, dropping me off at the pool for my training sessions before it opened to the public. I had to be at the office by 9:00 a.m., so that gave me a good couple of hours of swimming before I went to work each day.

I had by now established myself as a South Australian state champion in butterfly and breaststroke and had also begun serious training in backstroke and freestyle as part of a group of swimmers who were working on the individual medley swim, in which each quarter of a distance was swum in a different style.

The sports pages of *The Advertiser* called us "pioneers of the new generation of swimmers who are proficient in all strokes." Between us, my teammates and I held nearly all the state titles in senior and junior ranks.

The press called us the "Chrysler Club's galaxy of swimming stars."

Our mastering of all four strokes eventually led to the individual medley becoming a recognized swim event in competitions.

Local swimmers were gaining a new prestige in that year. Even winners of country events were now recognized with an actual inscribed medal instead of a dish or vase from a contributing retailer. I enjoyed receiving medals, but no medal would ever replace my ugly ceramic donkey or help me recollect the sweet memories of the playful camaraderie and youthful enthusiasm I'd encountered in my earliest days as an Aussie swimmer the way that donkey could.

Swimming in general was becoming more popular, and that summer, the Adelaide City Pool drew increasingly greater numbers of recreational swimmers, especially on weekends.

"It's too crowded," one of my fellow swimmers complained one day. "I can't train properly."

This had become a familiar refrain among club members and competitive swimmers at the pool recently.

"I'm sure they are all peeing in it," someone else joked. "You know we're swimming in a pool that is 80 percent urine."

We all moaned.

"It really is so crowded," I said to a teammate next to me. "Pee or no pee."

"Why don't you train in the Henley pool on weekends?" she suggested. "I do. It's saltwater. Some swimmers find it hard on their eyes, but it has the advantage of fewer people."

The Henley pool was one of the oldest pools in South Australia, opened in 1934 as a not-for-profit, open-air, saltwater pool at the edge of the sea, a fifteen-minute drive or short commuter train ride from the city. It was also home to one of Australia's oldest registered swimming clubs, the Henley and Grange Swimming Club.

"I have thought about it," I told her. "I've seen the pool. Love the beach location, but I have not swum in it yet. It might work for me on the weekends."

"I'm sure you'll like it," she said. "Maybe we can train together."

* *

Since I worked in the city not too far from the City Baths, the Adelaide pool was more convenient, of course, for my weekday training, but the following weekend, I hopped on the Sunday morning train to the saltwater pool at Henley Beach.

My teammate was right. It proved to be far less crowded than the city pool. It felt wonderful to be able to swim my laps without bumping into anyone, and I found that I did not mind the saltwater at all. I also loved the pool's proximity to the sea and the beach, where, after a couple-mile training session, I could spread out a towel on the warm sand, close my eyes, and let myself drift under the blue sky with the soft sounds of the gentle surf in my ears.

Soon, the Henley pool became my favorite hangout on weekends.

I had by this time discovered that I enjoyed long-distance swims. In competitive events, I was a slow starter—it took me a while to find my rhythm—but I had endurance and always had enough energy left at a long distance to increase my speed and sprint to the finish. The Henley Beach pool proved the perfect place to begin rigorous training for two long-distance events in which I hoped to participate soon: the annual 1-mile 200-yard Swim Through Adelaide in the Adelaide Torrens River and the 1-mile 600-yard Henley and Grange Jetty-to-Jetty Ocean Swim.

On some weekends, my father drove me to Henley. He observed my strokes, helped me see where I could improve, and timed my practice sessions. My mother was not a beach person, but my sister joined me frequently. An avid reader, she would lie on the beach reading a book while I trained in the pool.

Soon enough, this led to a new family acquisition.

Chapter 19
New Loki
Adelaide, South Australia, 1953

"I'll see you after you've swum your thousand miles," Laura joked as she left me at the pool to train for the upcoming Swim Through Adelaide. Skipping down the steps toward the beach, bag and towel slung over her shoulder, book in hand, she shouted, "Maybe I'll swim a mile in the ocean."

We both laughed.

"Sure," I yelled back, "but watch the sharks don't get you."

My eight-year-old sister, having been dragged by our parents to every one of my swim events in the past few years, would definitely not be a competitive swimmer. She would be a runner and an equestrian who would one day ride horses along the California seashore while watched by our proud father, the former Dutch cavalryman.

But even though we had different interests and were eight years apart in age, being the only two children of a tiny nuclear family of four that had begun a whole new life in a foreign land had forged a close bond between us. Having left behind a large extended family of aunts, uncles, and cousins when our parents brought us from Holland to Australia, our age difference was submerged by a mutual need for continuity. We depended on each other to maintain the fragile thread connecting us to the shared heritage that the Australian government demanded we renounce if we were to belong.

We enjoyed our beach time together in our individual ways. With their wide, sandy expanses and gentle, rolling surf, the beaches of Adelaide's nearby seaside suburbs—Henley, Grange, and Glenelg—were both a swimmer's and sunbather's paradise. After I had finished training for a couple of hours, I would usually find my sister stretched out on the sand with a favorite book, totally content.

Today, however, Laura came running toward me just as I was leaving the pool. With a voice bubbling over with excitement, she blurted out, "Henny, Henny. They are giving away puppies. Remember you promised to get me one? Henny, remember, when Loki died? Remember, in Ki Ki? You promised. You promised, Henny. Remember!?"

I remembered—of course I did. I remembered only too well the loss of our two last dogs. First, Beertje, who had to be left behind in Amsterdam. And then Loki, shot by an unknown person in Ki Ki.

My sister grabbed my hand and dragged me several hundred yards down the wide, sandy beach to where a skinny teenage boy in red shorts was seated cross-legged behind a large cardboard box. As we got closer, I saw a squirming heap of little black-and-white puppies who pleaded with their shiny black noses and soulful, dark eyes, "Please, please take me."

"How big is their mother?" I asked the boy, who looked to be about fourteen years old.

"Small; she's a terrier," he said.

"And the dad, do you know?" Then I naively added, "We can only take one if it's a small breed." My mom had stressed that we could have another dog, but only if it was small.

"Oh," said the smart boy, obviously having been sent to the beach to get rid of the unwanted litter, "I think he was a sausage dog. You know, a dachshund."

I narrowed my eyes. "Okay, the truth."

"Well, he was small," he insisted. "Very small. Like a dachshund."

By now, my sister had fallen in love with the pushiest puppy, who was licking her hand and climbing up her arm to be taken home, and of course, I couldn't resist that puppy either after I had held him. So we took our new Loki home on the train.

"Do you think his dad really was a dachshund?" Laura asked me as we walked to the station. "Aren't they usually brown?"

I shrugged. "I didn't see any brown puppies. But the boy should know, right?"

"Well, he said he was small like a dachshund. What really matters is that he was small, right?"

We agreed.

"What on earth?"

Our mother looked at Laura and me and the wriggling black-and-white pup in Laura's arms as we burst through the door, thrilled with our surprise. She looked concerned.

"His mother is a terrier and his dad a dachshund," I said quickly.

"He's small," Laura added. "You said we could have a small dog."

"He looks big for a puppy whose father is a dachshund," my mother said. "His legs and feet are too big."

"But he's so cute," my sister pleaded.

My mother didn't look convinced—but when the puppy reached up to her and put his front paws on her chest, I could see that he had found a new home.

Our new Loki was a remarkably smart and talented pup. Quickly housebroken, ready to respond to commands, he made sure to spread his affection among the four of us. We never formally decided on a name. There appeared to be an unspoken acceptance by all four of us that he was our new Loki, so Loki it was.

Only one problem: New Loki kept growing and growing and growing, until we had a long-legged, black-and-white mongrel almost the size of a Great Dane rambling through our two-bedroom suburban home. Fortunately, our Henley Beach puppy turned out to be a lovable if very large family dog, and our parents were remarkably sanguine about him.

Our dad joked from time to time, shaking his head, that "that must have been a gigantic dachshund."

"But please don't bring home any more surprises," my mom said, groaning, when I took off for my training sessions for the next competitive long-distance swim.

Chapter 20
Swim Through Adelaide
Adelaide, South Australia, 1954

"**G**ood on ya, mate, you did it!"

The jovial Aussie greeting rang in my ears above the cacophony of congratulations in various languages as I climbed out of the Torrens River with other swimmers who had just completed the 1-mile 200-yard Swim Through Adelaide. Parents and family members, including my mother, greeted us with towels and candy bars while they conversed and shared excitement in their different languages of origin.

Sports-loving Australians excelled at creating spectacular sporting events. The competitive swim I'd just completed through the Torrens River—or the Karrawirra Pari, as it is named in the Indigenous Kaurna language (the Kaurna people are the traditional owners and custodians of the Adelaide Plains)—was no exception. The annual summer event offered sports fans, friends, and families an opportunity to stroll along the banks of the river and observe and cheer on the hundred or more swimmers of all ages competing for the prized *Advertiser* Cup (and to watch famed Aussie surfers on ski patrols ensure the swimmers' safety). The festive atmosphere created a communal bonding and sense of belonging that celebrated Aussie sportsmanship in its best form.

While drying off, I tried to listen for the swim time and winner announcements and did not pay much attention to my parents' conversation with other parents and friends, some of whom had also migrated here in the past few years.

The city of Adelaide, capital of the State of South Australia, had in recent years become a magnet for increasing numbers of European immigrants. Stretched out between the rolling foothills of the Mount Lofty Ranges and the wide, sandy beaches of the Southern Ocean, Adelaide, with its spacious parks, wide avenues, and Mediterranean climate, offered an environment of peace, beauty, and abundance that spelled safety and hope for young migrant families.

"I think you swam one of your best times," my dad, holding up his stopwatch, said to me in English.

Before I could respond, a young blond man asked my dad a question, and he turned away to answer.

As they conversed, I heard familiar sounds—harsh, guttural—and stopped breathing. No. It wasn't possible! They were speaking German. How could he?

I had not heard the German language spoken in public since I was a little girl and the Nazis had controlled the streets of my Amsterdam. Hearing it now, my body recoiled as if recalling a physical beating. Images of black-booted soldiers in uniform—rifles slung over their shoulders, arms raised in a Heil Hitler salute, while they dragged helpless people out of their homes—flashed through my brain. My throat closed, and for a moment I had trouble catching my breath.

How could he? My own father?

"Henny, this is Werner," my dad said, introducing me to the neatly dressed, smiling young man in beige pants and a short-sleeved blue shirt standing next to him.

"Werner, this is Henny. My daughter. She is a state swimming champion." He said this in English and then in German with what sounded like fatherly pride.

I gasped, unable to respond. Had my father gone mad?

"Werner just arrived in Australia," my dad informed me. "He is also a swimmer."

The young blond man stuck out his hand and said in a heavy accent that made him almost impossible to understand, "I am pleased to meet you."

I ignored his hand, scowled at my father, turned my back, and walked away to where my mother stood chatting with friends and family of a Hungarian teammate. They were discussing the political situation in Eastern Europe, where Hungarians were being oppressed and displaced from their land by Russian aggressors. Ever since her involvement in the Resistance during the Nazi occupation in Amsterdam, my mother had retained a strong ongoing interest in European politics. My dad and I often teased her, "Most people cannot start their day without their morning coffee, but Mom cannot start hers without reading the daily morning newspaper."

I tried to get her attention. "Mom, why is Daddy speaking German to that guy?"

She looked puzzled.

It did not take my father long to catch up to me. "Why were you so rude to that boy?" he demanded.

"Wow, you don't know!?" I lashed out in anger. "You want me to be friendly with a German? You know what those Nazis did to us."

"Henny, the war is over," he reminded me. "Werner is only two or three years older than you. How old were you when the war ended?"

"You know I was seven."

"Right, so he was nine or ten. He was a child, like you."

I hesitated, for a moment taking in the fact of a German child on the other side of the trauma I had experienced. "Why did you have to speak German with him?"

"He is just learning English and doesn't understand it very well yet. I was trying to make him feel at home. He is alone, trying to make a new life for himself. You should understand what that's like." My dad looked me in the face, his eyes holding mine in a connection from which there was no escape. "Not everyone who speaks German is a Nazi."

My father, although Dutch, had been born in Germany, where his own father had worked for many years. As a little boy, he'd been fully bilingual—speaking Dutch at home, but conversing in German with playmates and at school. When he was seven years old, his father had lost his life in a work-related accident and his mother had taken the family back to Holland.

"It's hard to learn a new language, adapt to a new culture, and leave the past behind," my dad said. "You know that."

"Well, he should learn English. That's why we are here. To become Australians. You shouldn't encourage him to speak German," I said in a voice that I hoped would shame my father.

My mom joined our conversation. I could tell she had been listening.

"It's still frightening for Henny and me to hear German," she said to my dad. "You must understand that."

My dad nodded.

Then she turned to me, speaking Dutch, as she still always did with me. "Daddy is right," she said. "Not all Germans were Nazis. And remember that the Nazis who broke into our home and took Nel that night were Dutch men."

"It's going to take time," she said, looking at my dad. Then she turned back to me and said in her matter-of-fact way, "You don't have to be friends with the German boy, but you mustn't be cruel."

For a moment, the three of us stood suspended in our individual memories and experiences, all long buried or only partially healed.

"Hey," my dad suddenly said, "did you hear that? They just announced that you were the second fastest lady in the swim!"

It turned out that I had indeed recorded the second fastest time swum by a woman in the Swim Through Adelaide that year. A brief mention in the sports pages the following day would note my time as being especially "remarkable" because I had swum breaststroke the whole distance.

The fastest time for a woman was swum by one of my teammates, a girl who had migrated to Australia from Hungary.

I stepped over to congratulate her in the language we now shared and said laughingly, "Good on ya!"

She held out her hand. "I think we both swam well."

The next week, I saw Werner in the city pool at a training session. He waved and said, "Hello."

I gave a small wave back.

For the remainder of that summer, we would see each other in the pool now and then; each time, we said hello, nodded, and smiled. Then we swam, focusing on our strokes and turns.

Many of the boys and girls with whom I swam, whether in Adelaide City Pool, in the meandering Torrens River, or in the gently rolling waves off the shores of Adelaide's seaside suburbs, had experienced war and postwar violence and brutal political upheavals in their faraway childhood countries. But while our parents and their friends might be discussing the European political situation and the world's divided opinions, we did not talk about our traumatic pasts or the differences that had brought us and our families to Australia.

Instead, like global siblings, we immersed ourselves in the Australian waters that tested our young bodies, while endless sunshine promised futures of freedom and opportunity. We dove into the pool, the river, or the ocean, where we focused our minds and bodies on our united goal to be the best we could be. And when one of us won a race or even just finished with strength and determination, we used our Aussie-acquired "Good on ya!"—not only to show our support for one another, but also to assert our belonging in our new Australian lives.

"How could you swim in that polluted river?" friends, looking aghast, would ask me years later, when swimming in the Torrens River had long been banned because of pollution levels and health threats. But back in the early 1950s, swimmers of all ages who were registered with the South Australian Amateur Swimming Organization could not wait to dive into that river for the annual event. We changed into our swimsuits at the Adelaide City Baths and gathered at the Weir footbridge nearby, from which we dove into the river to swim the 1 mile and 200 yards. A handicapped race, it allowed slower swimmers to have an early start while faster swimmers were given a minute or more handicap. And when we reached the finish line at the Adelaide University Bridge, all swimmers were greeted with the jovial Australian "Good on ya, mate, you did it!" by friends, family, and spectators, no matter how fast or slow we had swum.

The Swim Through Adelaide provided me with a sense of community and celebrated the Aussie sportsmanship in which I had found a feeling of safety and belonging.

Chapter 21
Ocean Swims and Beauty Contests
Henley Beach, South Australia, 1954

On January 26 each year, Australians observed Australia Day. The day marked the 1788 landing of the first British convict ship in Sydney Cove, New South Wales, when the British flag was raised in present-day Australia. As awareness grew about the horrors perpetuated by white settlers on Australia's First Nations people, the day would eventually become one of controversy and mourning and be aptly renamed Invasion or Survival Day by many.

But as an immigrant Dutch girl in the early 1950s, I was at that time more acutely attuned to the suffering inflicted by the British rulers on the convicts and unwanted poor whom they had so cruelly exiled from England and shipped to an alien land on the other side of the world. Perhaps because I had been taken from my own country of origin, I identified a little with the exiles who celebrated their survival on Australia Day.

A national holiday, the day was observed with sports events and community gatherings throughout the country. In South Australia, the famed 1-mile 600-yard ocean swim between the Henley jetty and the Grange Beach jetty was a staple event of the area's Australia Day celebrations. A tradition that had begun in 1917 when the Henley and Grange Swimming Club held its first event, it continued to draw hundreds of swimmers each year.

I had signed up for the swim with a mixture of hope and trepidation. Placing second fastest woman in the Swim Through Adelaide had given me hope that I might have a chance to be first in the longer ocean swim. The race would be coed, though places and prizes were to be assigned by gender. Most of the swimmers swam freestyle, while my preferred long-distance stroke was still the traditional breaststroke. The breaststroke tended to be slower, but I knew it to be an efficient endurance stroke for distance swims.

The morning of the race, some hundred or more swimmers and I dove off the Henley Beach jetty and into the sea. We'd been warned that the waves were unusually choppy, and the first yards went slowly as we juggled for positions, but we soon found our individual rhythms.

The saltwater on my lips unexpectedly plunged me into a memory. I found myself going back to a time when my dad and I had eaten salted herring from one of the small stalls on a canal near our home in Amsterdam, just before we left for Australia. I could feel my dad's presence. He didn't care to swim in pools much, always preferring to swim in the open waters of rivers and seas. As a little boy, he had learned to swim in the Rhine River in Cologne, Germany. I knew he and my mom were driving to the Grange jetty right now, where, of course, they would be waiting to greet me at the finish line.

I looked around to note the swimmers in front of and behind me. I was off to a slow start, which was always my problem, but I soon found my speed. The water temperature felt like a Goldilocks mean: not so hot that it would make my heart rate race when I increased my speed, nor so cool that my body would have to use precious energy to warm itself. The great sea supported me, and the sky reached down to fill my lungs with each breath. I felt strong and strangely exhilarated.

The pain and cramps I had been experiencing during and between my periods recently had not been too bad this month. Yes, my body felt strong today. I belonged here in these waters Down Under, exactly at this time of my life.

As I stroked rhythmically through the choppy saltwater, I experienced a moment of Zen. I felt myself merge with all things above and below me—not knowing where my body ended and the water began, my breathing in tune with the air and in concert with all things living around me. A strange clarity permeated my mind. I was a part of all that transcended and held us together. I sensed that I was wearing a beatific smile.

A boat went by on or near the horizon. I barely glimpsed it, but when I did, I remembered that there had been a shark warning earlier that week. The race organizers had decided to ask several boat owners for assistance to ensure the safety of the swimmers.

I increased my speed but felt no fear. I silently said, "Thank you, Shark, for letting me swim in your home."

The distances between the swimmers had begun to widen. My stroke was steady, and two other strong female swimmers and I kept pace with one another. We passed some of the slower boys. Those of us who were more used to long distances steadily pulled ahead, maintaining our individual tempos.

Focus only on your stroke. Bend your elbows. Pull those arms a little deeper, faster. Thrust them forward. Breathe!

The Grange jetty came in sight. I kicked my legs into high gear and drew on all my energy reserves to increase my speed. Just a few hundred yards to go now.

No time to look around. No energy to waste. The rule was to

round the jetty, swim to the surf, and run up the beach to the finish line, which was monitored by the timekeepers.

Drawing on whatever reserves I had left, I pushed my body to a sprint through the last yards of the surf. My feet hit the sand. I tried to stand up, but my legs had turned into rubber. I stumbled.

Pull up those knees, push them through the water. Now run to that finish line on the beach. You are almost there!

Cheers from my parents and other well-wishers told me I had made it. My mother handed me a towel as I flopped down on the sand.

"First lady. Fastest woman. Fourth place overall. You beat most of the boys," my dad announced in a loud voice with a big grin on his face. Stopwatch in hand, as always.

As I recovered my breath, two of the Henley and Grange swim club swimmers sat on the sand next to me.

"Henny, we want you to represent the Henley and Grange in the Henley and Grange Carnival Bathing Beauty Contest," one of them said.

I laughed. "You're joking. No. Not ever. I am a swimmer, not a bathing beauty queen."

Another club member, a girl, joined the boys. "No," she insisted, "it's for the club. We've been talking and think you could win it for us. We've all agreed."

"No, I can't do that." I made a face. "I hate beauty contests. I don't support women being paraded around to be gawked at like circus animals." I bit into the chocolate bar my mom had handed me. "Women should be rewarded for our athletic ability, our intellect, our artistic work. Not for the way we look."

"It's just a carnival competition between the Sailing Club, the Angling Club, the RSL club (Returned Services League), and our swim club," one of the Henley and Grange coaches, now joining the conversation, wheedled. "It would mean a lot for the prestige of our club if we won."

Since I had been swimming more regularly in the Henley pool and made new friends there in the past year, I had been thinking of transferring my membership to the Henley and Grange club. Was I being unfair and unsportsmanlike, or even insulting, to my future club if I refused?

I turned to my parents, who had been listening to the ongoing conversation. "Is it rude to refuse?"

"What's wrong with acknowledging you are pretty?" My dad shrugged. "You would be representing the club you want to join."

I looked at my mom.

"Just enter to support the club," she said. "You do not need to win."

My mother's response sounded snarky to me. "You don't think I can win a beauty contest," I snarled back at her—then, spurred by that mother-daughter exchange, I turned to the others and said, "Yes, I'll do it."

Could I take back my words? No, it was too late. I had consented to parade around in a swimsuit in front of ogling strangers for the Carnival Queen competition in the Henley and Grange Carnival Bathing Beauty Contest. Results would be announced the following month.

For my 1-mile 600-yard ocean swim, I won a silver-plated trophy cup marked "Fastest Time (Lady)," and I was also given a casserole dish with a silver-plated stand inscribed "First Lady" with the date and distance. I never did find out if the "First Gentleman" was also given a casserole dish and stand.

Chapter 22
Working Girls
Adelaide, South Australia, 1954

"So do we address you as Your Highness?" Dot teased me as Jane did a little mock curtsy.

We were meeting for a milkshake at our favorite milk bar, on a lunch break from our respective jobs.

Dot and I had become friends when we were both students in business college. Blond, short, and bubbly, she had dreams of seeing the world and had set her hopes on becoming an air hostess with Pan American. "It will fulfill two goals," she said. "See the world and find a rich husband." It would have to be in that order, because air hostesses in the 1950s could not be married women.

Jane, who possessed a powerful operatic voice, was a fellow stenographer whom I had met through mutual friends. She was saving money to study singing in Italy.

The three of us had bonded over conversations about our individual plans to travel the world. It had been fun to discover that I shared a unique Australian trait with my Aussie girlfriends: We were all restless.

"Just stick a pin anywhere in the world map, I promise you'll find an Aussie who has either visited or is working there," Dot asserted.

Jane agreed. "If you are not restless, you cannot be an Australian."

"But tell us, Your Majesty," Dot said. "How was it?"

They both leaned forward, expectant looks on their faces.

"Don't know how I won." I shrugged. "I felt like such a fake, parading around in a swimsuit in front of those judges like a pampered poodle. I did decide to wear heels. I do have good legs. Answered a bunch of questions. Smiled a lot." I blew out a breath; I had mixed feelings about winning the Carnival Bathing Beauty Contest. "You know, I didn't do anything to earn it. It's not like winning a swim event for which I've trained hard. But I was glad to win for the swim club."

"Did the club have a float in the parade?" Jane asked.

"Yes, I was the Henley and Grange Carnival Bathing Beauty Queen, sitting on her throne on a float being paraded through the streets." My eyes widened. "I was wearing nothing but a swimsuit and waving at the people gathered at the curbs. Can you imagine!?"

Dot roared. "Did you do the queen's royal wave?"

I laughed. "Oh yes, and my loyal subjects bowed and cheered. Maybe I would have enjoyed my role more if I had worn a crown and a gorgeous gown!" I shook my head. "This queen can't even afford a new dress. I need to earn more money," I lamented.

I had been working at my job at the steel company for a couple of years now. My work was praised, and I was called regularly to take dictation from the owner of the company.

"You should demand a raise at work," Dot said. "You're being taken for granted. Women are always being taken for granted. We need to marry wealthy men or we are doomed."

Jane, more serious, agreed. "No harm in asking. I have been thinking of doing it myself."

Encouraged by my friends, the next day, I asked Brenda, our supervisor, if she would schedule an appointment with her boss. She asked me for my reason.

"I want a pay raise," I told her.

She grimaced. "That may be difficult, but I'll schedule a meeting."

She was always true to her word, and she and I met with her boss, Mr. Randall, for our meeting that very afternoon.

"I hear you want an increase in your wages," he said after I sat down in the chair opposite his desk. "You know, we took a risk hiring you. You had only been in Australia for a short time. In a way, we furthered your education. We helped you perfect your English and your shorthand and typing skills. You were hired as a stenographer, but now you have the skills of a secretary."

I nodded in agreement. "That's why I want to be paid more. I don't want to be just a stenographer anymore. I want to be a personal secretary."

I pointed to Brenda. "I want her job."

Both Mr. Randall and Brenda looked surprised but laughed.

"Well, you can't have her job," Mr. Randall said.

My face flushed a bright red, betraying my insecurity. I stammered, "No, I did not mean that. I want a job like the one she has. I want to be a personal secretary like Brenda."

Mr. Randall smiled. "I understand. You are a talented girl. You may have gone as far as you can go here with us. We would like you to stay, but we do not have another secretarial position available, and we cannot pay you more than we are paying the other stenographers."

He thought for a moment. "I have a friend who runs a successful advertising company. I think they are looking for a personal secretary for one of their sales managers. We will be sad to lose you, but I am sure that with the references we can give you, he will offer you a salary that will please you. Think about it. Maybe talk it over with your parents."

I nodded and stumbled out of his office.

He was right. In some sense, working with the girls at the steel company under the supervision of Brenda's firm kindness had been a continuing education for which I had been paid.

It would be hard to leave the friends I'd made, but I decided to go for the interview.

A week later, my letter of recommendation in hand, I nervously stepped into the carpeted offices of an advertising agency on Rundle Street in downtown Adelaide.

An attractive, long-legged girl my age with startling violet-blue eyes and wavy, shoulder-length, reddish-brown hair welcomed me at the reception desk. "You must be Henny de Vries." She smiled. "Mr. Sanders is expecting you. Just come with me."

I nodded and smiled before nervously following her down a long corridor into a windowless, wood-paneled office.

A handsome, middle-aged man, his dark brown hair sleeked down with pomade, motioned for me to sit down on the other side of his extremely large desk and waved away the receptionist. "So, Miss de Vries, you are applying for the secretarial position?"

I smoothed my skirt over my thighs. "Yes, I am, sir."

He looked at me and down at the letter I handed him. "Well, you were certainly given a glowing recommendation by your previous employer. It says here that you speak excellent English. You have only been in Australia a few years. How did you manage that?"

"I had already learned basic English in high school in Amsterdam before we emigrated," I responded, deciding not to mention Lyceum, since that seemed to confuse people sometimes.

"Why do you want to be a personal secretary?" he asked.

I had anticipated that question and responded with the answer I had practiced: "I like being responsible and creative. I think a good secretary can support and help her boss do his best possible work. I'm good at shorthand, I'm a fast typist, and I enjoy challenges."

Mr. Sanders smiled. "Your English is indeed very good. So, what are your dreams and hopes for your own future?"

I had not expected that question and had to think for a moment before answering, "To be the best person I can possibly be." I immediately felt that was the most foolish answer I could have given.

He laughed.

We chatted for a few more minutes. By the end of the conversation, I felt uncertain as to whether I would be hired. Before I could ask him, he stood up, shook my hand, and said, "You'll be advised of the firm's decision by mail," then called his shapely receptionist back into the office to see me out.

She led me back down the corridor. As we reached the exit door, she whispered, "I'm sure you have the job. Our bosses here like pretty girls."

I was too naive to register the red flag in her comment.

Chapter 23
You Asked for It
Adelaide, South Australia, 1954

A heavyset man with the wide-shouldered appearance of an Australian rugby player and close-set eyes above a bulbous nose, my new boss had short, pudgy hands and fingers that stroked my arm or shoulder every time he addressed me. Thin strands of blond hair covered his shiny, balding head. He did not smile much.

He set me to work as his assistant almost immediately. I was to take dictation, answer calls, and help him organize appointments and advertising information.

I'd received my formal acceptance letter in the mail a week after my interview. It told me that I had been assigned the position of personal secretary and assistant to one of the firm's senior sales representatives. I had been thrilled to learn that I would be working within walking distance of the milk bar where my friends and I liked to meet.

Though I did not take immediately to my new boss, the work itself absorbed me. I enjoyed having more responsibility, and the increased salary allowed me to replenish my wardrobe with a new sleeveless summer dress, a pair of high-heeled pumps, and a bright fuchsia lipstick that my mother didn't approve of.

* *

Filled with confidence for the next grown-up phase of my life, I was surprised when the matronly woman in charge of advertising layout, Miss Jones, reprimanded me for my choice of dress and lipstick when I returned from my next milkshake lunch with Dot and Jane.

"Are you saying that my boss won't approve?" I asked.

"He may like it a bit too much," she said. "You young girls just think you can flaunt it."

I didn't know how to respond and retreated to my office cubicle adjoining hers. It was an exceptionally hot day, but the work kept me occupied. By the end of the day, I was running late and hurrying to finish up the last of the letters I needed to type.

Everyone except my immediate boss had already left by the time I walked into his office and handed him the letters.

He looked up at me. "You look very pretty today. New dress?"

I nodded yes, smiled, and was about to step out of his office when he got up from behind his desk and walked toward me.

"Just a moment." He put his hand on my arm. "I just want to tell you. You are doing a good job."

His hand moved up my arm to my shoulder. I froze. What was he doing?

He pushed me against the wall with his left arm. His face close to mine, his right hand pulled at the top of my sleeveless dress and moved over my breast.

"You have lovely breasts. But you know that, don't you?"

I could feel his breath on my face. With a rough shove, he forced my body harder against the wall, the full length of his body pinning mine. I could hardly breathe.

"What are you doing?" I tried to push back, but he was too heavy.

His eyes looked hard and cruel. His hand pinched my breast. The full weight of his body kept pressing. I could not breathe. I wanted to scream, but my voice would not come out. I could not utter a sound.

His hand fumbled inside my dress, his fingers in my bra, his body trapping me against the wall. He pushed his face against mine and moved his mouth over my cheek and ear. "You are so beautiful. Too beautiful."

I was a strong young woman, a competitive swimmer, but I felt frozen by an inexplicable paralysis. I could not speak or move. A feeling of utter helplessness and fear overcame me. This wasn't happening!

I would ask myself for a long time after this occurred, *Why did I not fight him? Why did I not kick and scream? For heaven's sake, I was a champion swimmer.*

Suddenly, I burst into tears and heard myself sobbing, "You have a wife and a little girl."

He stepped back and in a raised, angry voice exclaimed, "You know this is your fault! You asked for it. You are to blame. Wearing that dress. You know it." His face and balding head had turned a dangerous red.

I may have said "I'm sorry"; I'm not sure. What I do know is that I ran out of the office, and as I grabbed my purse off my desk, he yelled after me, "This was your fault. You know, you should be ashamed of yourself!"

I stumbled out of the office building, wondering if it really was my fault. Feelings of shame and reproach flooded me. *You are weak. Why did you not fight back?*

This helpless girl who could not fight back was not the woman I had thought myself to be.

"You are lucky to be your mother's daughter," my mom's friends from the Resistance in Amsterdam had always told me. "Your mother is courageous, strong, and smart. You are like her."

Maybe I was not like my mom. Maybe I was weak and cowardly.

I had always been rewarded for my strength. I was the "brave girl" during the war, a "champion" in the pool, a "smart girl" for my good grades in the classroom. I did not know how to deal with the feelings of this shaky, weak crybaby who had burst into tears.

I somehow got myself to the pool that afternoon, although I would never remember how I got there or even being in the locker room and changing into my swimsuit. I must have been numb when I dove into the water. I recall the sensation of the cool water hitting my face and my tears mixing with water.

I turned my head sideways and forced my arms and legs to swim freestyle, my most challenging stroke at that time. *Harder, faster,* I told myself, and I forced my legs to kick with greater vigor and my arms to pull more quickly as I pushed myself to the end of the pool, where I flipped into the familiar butterfly and coursed half the lane without breathing.

My lungs exploded with rage when I finally took a breath.

I continued to swim, pushing harder and harder till I felt the surge of strength come back into my arms and legs. *Breathe, kick, you are a swimmer!* the voice inside me screamed.

Slowly, as the energy returned to my body, I began to recognize myself again.

Eventually, spent, I climbed out of the pool, got dressed, and went home.

I wasn't sure how to tell my parents that evening that I would not go back to that office. It seemed as if I was always telling them I would not do this or that.

"You're unusually quiet tonight," my mother remarked after dinner.

It was the opening I needed. With a faltering voice, I recounted what had happened at work that afternoon.

My parents listened with horror on their faces.

"Did he hurt you?" my mom asked. "Did he do anything else?"

"No, Mommy, I'm fine," I reassured her. "Honestly. Nothing else happened."

"That bastard!" my dad fumed. "Don't you worry. I'll go tomorrow and make sure he gets fired from that company."

"I'm not going back to work there," I said.

"No, of course not," my mom assured me. Then she turned to my dad. "I don't think we should do anything. Henny's name is regularly in the sports pages of the newspaper. She is the 'migrant' or 'Dutch' girl. We are New Australians. He's the Australian. It's his word against hers. He can destroy her reputation in the swimming world—ruin her life. She's too young for this."

"That man needs to be fired," my dad argued.

"It may have been my fault, Daddy," I said. "Miss Jones—you know, the layout person? She is an older woman, and she warned me about my lipstick and dress. She said the girls in our office were 'flaunting it.'"

My dad paused.

"I shouldn't have worn my new dress and that lipstick," I said.

"No matter what you wore," my dad insisted, "it was not your fault. He is a boss, a grown man, and he could have just told you not to wear that dress in the office. There is no excuse ever for a man to touch you against your will. Remember that." He turned to my mother. "I still think I need to write a letter to the company to warn them that their office environment is not safe for young girls."

"Please let it be, Daddy," I pleaded with him. "I'm okay."

He never told me whether he wrote the letter or not, but I did not return to that office. He found me a temporary job typing invoices in the joinery workshop of a friend of his.

I spent the next couple of weeks in the pool and the ocean, where life felt uncomplicated and I felt safe, even if there were sharks in the water.

But the pool would be closing for the winter months soon.

Chapter 24
The Winter Months
Adelaide, South Australia, 1954

With the pool closed for the winter months, my friendships with the girls my age outside of the swim world received more time and attention. Dot, Jane, and I met regularly for our favorite milkshakes at the milk bar on Hindley Street. Young and innocent, we shared our hopes and dreams for the future, looking for reflection and affirmation in one another.

We recognized that life for women in the 1950s was extremely constricting in Australia. Girls were expected to marry and become mothers. Careers were seen as temporary, and dreams were often short-lived. Birth control was not easily available to unmarried women. Girls got pregnant. Married women were not welcomed in most workplaces. Girls projected their dreams on the boys they fell in love with, and smart girls married boys who could manifest their dreams of success.

My dream had been to one day work in the newsroom of a newspaper, where stories were written and polished to go out into a world of eager readers—but any time I shared that dream with parents of friends or other adults I encountered, I was told, "Girls do not belong in the newsroom," followed by the friendly admonition, "Why are you worrying about a career? Pretty girl like you, you will be married and having babies in no time."

I went to the milk bar one winter afternoon not long after I'd quit my job to meet with Dot, Jane, and a new addition to our group, Helen.

Helen had dreams of becoming a model. We all agreed she already looked like one. At age eighteen, she was an elegant, slender, five-foot-ten beauty with flawless skin, high cheekbones, green eyes, and long auburn hair. But she said she had to hide her dreams from her parents, who wanted her to marry and give them grandchildren.

"I really don't want to get married or have children," she confided today as if sharing a deep sin. "I want to go to New York and be a model."

I shared that my maternal grandmother had wanted to be a writer and theologian but had instead ended up married with eleven children, ten of whom she'd raised to be adults. She always told her daughters that if they really wanted to marry and have children, they should limit it to two.

"I would have liked your grandma," Helen said. "I really can't see myself as a mother."

Dot had a boyfriend, Brian. She loved him. They had talked of marriage, but it conflicted with her dream to see the world. She still planned to become an air hostess on international flights.

"It's so unfair." She sighed. "Men can marry and still have careers. We can't. And I certainly can't afford to get pregnant. That's what happened to my mother, and she never let me forget that she had to give up her career because she had me. And I can't be married if I want to be a stewardess."

The airlines stipulated that their stewardesses be single women of a certain weight, height, and age. Even widows or divorced women were denied. It seemed marriage made us spoiled goods for the airline industry—and other venues on the ground and in the air as well.

"So, Henny, what happened with your new job?" Jane asked. She remained focused on her singing career. She devoted all spare time outside of work to voice lessons and was now seriously pursuing schools in Milan for operatic training.

When I told them what had happened, Dot said, "I'm not supposed to talk about this, but one of my cousins worked for a boss who stuck his fingers up inside her panties. She bled, because she was a virgin, but he told everyone she lied and that she'd done it to herself to try to make him leave his wife. And they believed him."

I asked, horrified, "What happened to your cousin? Is she alright?"

Dot shrugged. "I don't know. We don't talk much. I feel bad, because even I sometimes wondered if she made it up or wanted him to do it."

"That's horrible," I said, aghast. "I know I certainly didn't want to have old bald head's pudgy fingers fondle my breast!"

The four of us laughed and slurped our strawberry and caramel milkshakes, but I was aware of the presence of a cautioning shadow that challenged our innocent teenage bravado.

Perhaps out of a desire to find safety that winter, I occasionally joined my mother when she went to her Congregational Church service on Sundays. One of her friends had a son whom I had never met. He wanted to be a professional dancer, my mom said.

"So, you are our famous champion swimmer." A tall, stern-looking woman grabbed my hand one Sunday. "I'm Mrs. Webber. Your mother says that you are needing activity while the swimming pool is closed for the winter months. I think you should meet my son. James is looking for a dance partner. His dance classes are on Wednesday and Friday nights. He will come pick you up."

I guess I looked a little taken aback, because she squinted at me. "Alright?"

"Sure," I said. I actually didn't feel so sure, especially since I didn't know how to dance, but Mrs. Webber did not seem like the kind of person who would take my "no" for an answer.

"And, who knows," my mom said, "it might be fun—and good exercise for the next few months!"

When the doorbell rang and I opened the door the following Wednesday, I gaped.

"I'm James." Tall, slender, and dashing, with a thick head of wavy, strawberry blond hair and a sculpted profile that made him look like the American actor/dancer Danny Kaye, the young man at the door sported long eyelashes that fringed his soulful eyes and would certainly be the envy of every girl. With the flair of a movie star, he tossed a long white scarf around his neck and shoulders and said, "Shall we go?"

He pointed to a shiny white Holden parked in front of our house.

"Nice car," I said. "My dad also drives a Holden."

He shrugged. "It's my father's."

The hall where the dance classes took place was only a short ride away, which did not give us much time to get to know each other beyond establishing the already known fact that our mothers attended the same church.

The class was just about to begin when we arrived on the dance floor.

"I don't know how to dance," I told James.

"It doesn't matter, I'll teach you," he said. "Just follow my lead."

He laughed at my initial hesitation, put his hand on my waist, and counted, "One, two, three; one, two, three."

Suddenly, he pulled me close and whirled me around the floor. I stepped on his toes a few times, but he masterfully shifted my legs with his, held me close, and spun me until I was dizzy and breathless.

"You're a good teacher," I said, laughing. My admiration was genuine.

"I know," he responded.

As the weeks went by, my body began to respond instinctively and with increased pleasure to the attention that dance, like swimming, demanded from my every move. I responded not only to James's lead but also to the music and felt the rhythm that guided us both. I began to look forward to our Wednesday and Friday evenings. Soon we added Saturday practices to our weekly routine.

"Good, you are following me better," James would say, smiling, and hold me in such a way that our bodies merged and moved as one. And when I missed a step, he whispered in my ear, "Remember you have a dancer in you. She knows how to follow my lead."

As he improved his own dancing, we enjoyed our personal improvisations of a variety of classic dance routines that winter, but unfortunately, summer would soon be upon us.

"James," I reminded him after one of our Friday dances, "the pool opens in a few weeks. I will have to start my swim training then, so you'll need to find another dance partner."

"No, you can't do this," he responded with hurt and anger in his voice. "You are my partner. Did you just use me to learn to dance?"

"I warned you that I could only be your dance partner for the winter months and I had to focus on my swimming when the pool opened again," I defended myself.

"But you let me believe that dancing had become important to you," he said. "We are so good together."

"We are, and I love dancing with you, but my swimming is as important to me as your dance is to you. I'm a champion swimmer." I tried to impress my side of things on him. "I hope to be training for the Nationals this summer. Do you really expect me to give that up for your dancing?"

"I can't find another dance partner." James raised his voice. "I have spent all these months teaching you."

"I told you that I would start swimming again in September," I said, getting annoyed now. "You just didn't want to hear me."

"You told me you looked forward to our dances. I believed we had a partnership. You just wasted my time. I don't have time to find another partner before the dance competitions begin!" he yelled.

Hurt and angry as well, I raised my voice to match his: "I did love our dancing together, but my swimming championships are more important to me."

"Oh, so it's all about you and your swimming. You're just selfish. You just used me!" He almost spat the words at me, his beautiful face scrunched up in rage.

Shocked and hurt, I yelled back, "I'm selfish? You're the selfish one. It's all about you and your dancing. You refuse to understand that my swimming is important to me."

Trembling, I turned my back on him and walked away. He did not attempt to stop me, as I think I hoped he would.

James and I might have sorted out our differences and remained friends, but any chance we had at reaching a mutual understanding was destroyed when his mother told some people at the church that my mother had raised a daughter who was "selfish, ungrateful, and didn't know her place."

"She needs to be reminded that she is just a New Australian," Mrs. Webber told them. "She should be thankful to my son that he picked her, a migrant, to be his dance partner."

Upon learning this, according to other church members, my mother picked up her umbrella, shook it at James's mother, and told her she'd better not hear her say a bad word about me to anyone ever again.

When I told Dot, Jane, and Helen about the incident over our next milkshake, they laughed hysterically at the image of my mother shaking her umbrella at James's mother outside the church.

"Actually," I said, "I think she went to her house."

"No!" They roared with laughter. "Good on her. Good on your mum."

"Men never take anything we do seriously," Dot said.

And Helen, the most worldly among us, added, "Men always think their activities are more important than ours, and when we marry, we are expected to give up everything and become their cooks and cleaning ladies and coddle them the way their mothers did."

"Well, I'm not giving up my singing for anyone," Jane said.

But I wondered. "Maybe it would be different if you loved someone very much," I offered.

At that, Helen laughed at us. "Oh, you are all so naive."

I still felt sad about the way things had ended with James—and I couldn't wait for the pool to open. Life always felt so much simpler when I was swimming, and I knew the excitement and demands of the upcoming summer months would claim all my attention.

Chapter 25
Changes and Champions
Adelaide and Henley Beach, South Australia, 1955

"Did you hear?"
"Are you sure?"
"Yes, it's true."

Adelaide City Pool was abuzz with the exciting news that Harry Gallagher, the famed Sydney coach of Australia's fastest swimmers, was moving to South Australia and about to take over the management of the Adelaide City Baths, which included the city pool in which we regularly trained.

"He'll bring big changes with him, for sure. Have you heard? We'll be training with Dawn Fraser."

"She's moving here with him?"

"That should improve our times."

We twittered among ourselves like flocks of birds on a telephone wire.

Coach Gallagher, along with Dr. Frank Cotton and Forbes and Ursula Carlile (of a slightly earlier time), was regarded as a pioneer in sport science; he used a methodological approach to sports that introduced heart monitoring, interval and weight training, and other scientific methods and rigors to swim training.

Whether it was Harry's fame or just the progress of time, the next couple of years brought big changes for competitive swimmers in South Australia. Suddenly, we found ourselves training and competing with the fastest swimmers in the world: Dawn Fraser, the Australian swimming superstar, who moved to Adelaide with Harry, and Jon Henricks, the blonde human fish from Sydney, who now began to spend more of his time in Adelaide.

Adding to our excitement was the anticipation of Australia's National Swimming Championships, which were to be held in our serene, tranquil city that year. It would give all of us the opportunity to watch the country's fastest swimmers compete and witness the reveal of the champions who would no doubt represent Australia at the Olympics in Melbourne the following year.

"The photographer is waiting," a voice from outside the Henley Beach Club locker room called out to me.

After training intensely in the Adelaide City Pool during the week, I enjoyed being back in my less crowded saltwater pool on the edge of the sea on weekends.

I put on a navy-blue jacket with the official coat of arms of South Australia on its pocket, adjusted my calf-length gray skirt, and took one last look in the mirror before I stepped out into the sun.

"Ah, there you are. Step over here. Yes, the lady in the middle. The two gentlemen on either side. Good."

The three of us—Tony, Brian, and I—chuckled as we obeyed the serious young man who was arranging us for the official photo shoot.

"Two gentlemen and the lady in the middle," I mimicked, enjoying the camaraderie with my peers.

The three of us had placed well in the recent State Championships and would be representing not just the State of South Australia in the upcoming Australian National Swimming Championships but also our Henley and Grange club by the sea.

I felt honored, but not as confident as I should have. I had managed to win the state 220-yard breaststroke championship, which secured me a place in the Nationals, but I had placed second in both the 110-yard butterfly and 110-yard breaststroke. Of course, my body had always preferred the longer-distance swims, but I was also being challenged by an official change in the butterfly kick.

Competitive butterfly swimmers were now using a different leg kick that increased their speed. Called the dolphin kick, it required a swimmer to move their legs in a dolphin's-tail motion rather than the old breaststroke scissor kick that I had been used to. The new stroke seemed to come naturally to some of the friends I swam with, but I struggled to master it.

In addition, my menstrual periods were lasting longer these days, and at times, I did not seem to recover my usual strength and energy when swimming my training laps. I was aware that I would have to train hard if I wanted to do well in the prestigious Nationals.

"I have been asked to also take some photos of you in your bathing suit for the official records," the photographer said. "Do you mind?"

I shook my head. No problem—I'd planned to change into my swimsuit anyway, hoping to swim another hour or so before meeting my family and friends on the beach for a late afternoon picnic.

Since I had transferred from the Chrysler Club at the City Baths to the Henley and Grange club, my weekend swims had also turned into family-and-friends' social occasions. It had become a ritual for my family and various club members to gather on Sunday afternoons, post training, for snacks and chats on the sand.

The Henley and Grange swimmers had welcomed and embraced my whole family. The boys especially enjoyed the company of my dad, who regularly clocked my swims and regaled everyone with stories about the time he saw the American swimmer and actor Johnny Weissmuller, of Tarzan fame, swim in the Olympics that were held in Amsterdam in 1928. He loved to tell them how he had taken a job as an usher in the stands just so he could see his hero swim. Several of the boys soon persuaded him to be their unofficial timekeeper, as he was for me.

My sister continued to enjoy her time on the beach with her books and even managed to corral my mother into coming on Sundays. My mother made sure we had a real family picnic those days, complete with sandwiches and carafes of coffee.

Many times, our gatherings on the beach turned into wild discussions that focused not just on our swimming ambitions but also our education, work, or career plans, and even our broader dreams for the lives we hoped to create.

"I am planning to learn how to repair washing machines and refrigerators," one of the boys, Len, told my father one day. "Electric appliances are a thing of the future. Maybe I'll even open a shop one day and sell them." He looked at me. "And then I'll marry Henny."

My dad looked amused. "Oh, does she know that?"

I laughed. "No!"

A girl who had also recently joined the club said, "Well, I'm going to the university. I want to teach."

"That's good—you must teach English to migrants," my mother responded in her instructor tone of voice that always annoyed me.

"But first we must all cheer for Tony, Henny, and Brian when they swim in the Nationals," Len said. "They'll be representing Henley and Grange."

"Good thing the Nationals will be in Adelaide this year, so we will all be able to be there," one of the girls cried out. "You will make us proud, Henny."

"I hope so," I said.

"You know we will all be there cheering for you."

I was going to need to swim the best race of my life at the Nationals—not just for myself but also for every girl swimmer in my club. The weekend swims and beach gatherings reminded me of the confidence that had been placed in me, a confidence that lately did not always hold up. I would be representing the State of South Australia and needed to win—not only for the state but also for my beloved club at the edge of the sea.

I increased the intensity of my training schedule. I tried to ignore the times in the pool when I could not seem to access the strength and enthusiasm I had taken for granted since I had started swimming competitively as a little girl in Amsterdam, when my mother liked to tell me, "I realized that you would never be a runner like I was, but I saw that you liked to swim, and I saw that you could swim fast."

We had barely survived the war, and I always thought my mother believed swimming might help me forget the traumas she and I had experienced during those dark times, though I didn't remember her ever actually saying so.

When I showed her the photo of me, Brian, and Tony in our official jackets, she beamed. "Look at you. You are a champion representing South Australia in the Australian National Swimming Championships. If you do well, you may even represent Australia in the Olympics."

I heard the pride in her voice and hoped I could live up to it.

Chapter 26
Female Issues and "Secondhand Goods"
Adelaide, South Australia, 1955

"Damn!" I cried out loud.

The sharp pain woke me up before the alarm clock could. I sat up in bed, crossed my arms over my abdomen, and began the rocking movement that eased the pain. I felt the blood on the inside of my thighs. *Oh no, not again!*

I had been training hard each day for the National Swimming Championships, which were now right upon us. Excited and honored to be representing the State of South Australia, I tried to ignore the feeling that my body, which had always made me feel strong and confident, had lately turned against me. But my periods had been more frequent of late and lasted longer every time. I could not continue to ignore the excruciating cramps in the hope they would just disappear.

"Damn!" Once again, there was no way I would be able to make it to the crucial swim practice I needed to attend to be ready for the Nationals in just a few weeks.

My mother entered the room just as Laura, in the other bed, woke up.

"Are you okay?" my mother asked.

"I'm fine." I glared at her. Why did she never bother to knock on the door of our bedroom? "It's just my period."

"You should not be having them this often and for so many days." She frowned. "As soon as you are able, we are going to take you to the doctor."

"Oh, for heaven's sake, I can take myself to the doctor. I'm seventeen years old."

She left the room. I heard her tell my dad that he would not be driving me to swim practice before work that day.

"Female problems?" he asked. Having grown up the youngest brother with four sisters, my dad had no problem discussing female issues.

I felt sad that we would miss our drive to the pool again. Our times together were special to me, even though most of the time we hardly spoke a word. Neither of us being early morning people, we enjoyed our shared automobile bubble of mutual silence away from my mom, whose cheerfulness when the sun had barely risen made me want to scream at her and made my dad step outside for his first cigarette of the day.

I dressed and joined them in the kitchen. My mother poured me a cup of the hot tea that she steeped in a large earthenware teapot on the kitchen table. Dad sat reading the morning newspaper as he ate his usual oatmeal.

"Men are lucky," I said accusingly.

He smiled. "In some ways, yes, I guess you are right."

"I can't go to swim practice," I said.

"Maybe you should stay home from work also," he suggested.

I frowned. "Mom says I should see the doctor."

"Probably a smart idea," he said, returning to his newspaper.

I walked into the bedroom, hoping I could find enough pads to stem the menstrual flow. Tampons had not made it into the South Australian stores yet.

The cramps continued; I decided I really should skip work.

How could I prepare for the Nationals if I was doubled over with pain and bleeding two or more weeks out of the month?

Today I just wanted to stay in bed and sleep, but I agreed to make an appointment to see the doctor next week.

The doctor's office lay within walking distance of our home, and on the day of the appointment, my mother insisted on accompanying me. We were the first to arrive in the windowless waiting room; we sat down on two of the straight-backed wooden chairs arranged in a line along the wallpapered wall to wait. At least the yellow sunflowers and daisies on the beige wallpaper brought some light into the room.

A gray-haired nurse with a sweet, grandmotherly smile took down my information and assured me that the doctor would be "only a little while, dear. It's nice that your mum is here with you."

My mom patted my hand while we waited, a gesture that the twisting moods that turned me inside out these days processed with annoyance. Why did she still treat me like a child?

When the nurse called me, she said sweetly, "Your mum can come in with you, dear."

I shook my head, put my palm facing up toward my seated mom, and said in the sharpest tone I could muster, "No, my mother will wait."

I stepped into the room, where the doctor, a man the age of my father with sharp features in an unsmiling face, told me to undress and lie down. He pointed to a table with stirrups that made me think of images I'd seen of medieval torture chambers. When I was lying down, he put his hand on my belly, told me to breathe, and began to pelt me with questions about my activities.

"You are a competitive swimmer?"

"Yes, Doctor."

"How often do you swim?"

"Every day, if possible."

"How much every day?"

"About three or four miles," I said, trying to answer as truthfully as I could.

"Are you telling me that you swim three or four miles every day? Sounds to me like you are overdoing it, young lady. You know you are a girl, right?"

The accusatory tone of his voice made it sound like I had done something bad. His fingers prodded and kneaded the external parts of my belly. I yelped with the shock of the pain when he pushed down hard on the left side.

He frowned. "Put your feet in the stirrups so I can examine you."

As he stuck his head somewhere between my legs, I looked up at the ceiling of the room, wishing I could disappear.

Suddenly, his head reappeared above my knees. "You are a virgin; I can't examine you," he said abruptly. "We don't want to make you secondhand goods for your future husband, do we?" He stripped off his gloves and sighed. "You can get up and get dressed. I think you're just fine. It's normal for girls and women to experience cramps during menstruation and in the middle of the month. I suggest you go easy on the swimming. Too much exercise is not good for women. Rest up when you have your period, drink hot tea, and take a Bex powder every few hours."

Bex powders, dissolved in tea, were an Australian medicinal icon in the 1950s. Recommended for a wide variety of aches and pains such as headaches and backaches, the powders were lauded for their "calming effect" and predominantly prescribed to women. The cure for any female issue at that time was best expressed in the popular slang expression that all she needed was "a cup of tea, a Bex, and a good lie-down."

Several years after my doctor made sure I would "not be secondhand goods for a future husband," I almost hemorrhaged to death because of undiagnosed ovarian cysts. Fortunately, I was by then no longer a virgin. My life, and even one part of one remaining ovary, would be saved by a kind and competent surgeon. Twenty years after that, Bex powders would be revealed to cause severe kidney disease and be taken off the market for good.

But that year, when I was seventeen, Bex powders stirred into gallons of hot tea were my best friends. They eased the physical pain and discomfort of my disabling cramps and the erratic timing of my monthly cycles.

Meanwhile, I kept on swimming, because that's what I loved to do, and in the pool, I felt safe.

In sports-loving Australia, the strength and speed of my body in the water had given me an identity and a sense of belonging. I was a champion swimmer. If I was not that, then who would I be?

Chapter 27
You Are an Impostor!
Adelaide, South Australia, 1955

Camera lights flashed in our eyes. Newspaper sportswriters pelted us with questions. Officials, friends, and family surrounded the champions with hugs and congratulations. Winners of the final event kissed and splashed one another in the water.

This year's National Championships were over, and Australia's fastest swimmers had shown us who they were. Some of them would join the ranks of Olympians the following year.

I climbed out of the pool and walked alone to the locker room. The room stood empty, a rare phenomenon.

I sat on one of the benches and felt the tears rise in my eyes even as I fought hard not to let them come to the surface. I had let my state and my swim club down. I had let myself down. An inner voice of shame mocked the sobs I could not control: *You lost. You are not that strong girl everyone sees. You are an impostor, just not good enough, a loser.*

Strange how utterly alone we can be when fame has shifted to others. My sobs echoed off the gray metal lockers in the cavernous emptiness that seemed to mock my disappointment. The echo deepened my shame. I would not be seen as a candidate who would be training for the Olympic Game trials, as so many of my admirers had predicted. I had disappointed everyone.

Did the locker room always feel so cold and lonely for those who did not win? I shivered. Now what would I do?

My body, which had always made me feel so strong and safe in the water, had betrayed me. My identity was all tied up with being a swimming champion. A winner, not a loser. How could I face the world now?

I had been chosen to represent South Australia in the Nationals, competing in the 220-yard breaststroke and the 110-yard butterfly. "If you swim well in the Nationals," I'd been told, "you will be on your way to next year's Nationals and training for the Olympics in Melbourne."

But right from the first start, I'd been slow off the block, and no matter how hard I'd pushed in that first swim, I could not make up the time I had lost. My legs felt like lead. Where was the joy I'd always felt in a competitive swim?

I'd had my second chance today, a couple of days after the first event, but again I'd failed to find the energy in my body that brought speed, strength, and pleasure. I'd made the finals but not placed in either of the events in which I had participated.

Everything felt so wrong. My parents, teachers, and coaches had always praised me for my strength, courage, determination, and intelligence. "Henny was the bravest girl in the war years," my mother would often say with pride. But it was not me but my mother who was brave. I had not even fought back the boss who'd groped my breast with his pudgy fingers. I had cried instead. Lately, I could not access that person everyone else around me saw and valued.

"With your determination, stroke, and strength, you will make Australia proud in the next Olympics," teammates, friends, and family had told me.

"Of course, you will swim for the Netherlands," my uncles and cousins in Holland had written when I was only fifteen.

But no, I would not represent either country.

My physical strength and mental determination had been failing me this summer. A deep fatigue followed my long, painful menstrual cycles. I'd jump in the pool and tell myself, *You can do this. Come on, you're a champion. You are just being lazy.* But my legs refused to kick with the force needed for competition, and my sluggish body just wanted to go to sleep in the water.

Another doctor's visit had yielded only the advice to rest more and swim less, and a warning to my parents that the fatigue their daughter was experiencing was probably "female nerves" due to the "unnatural stress of the extreme competition" they encouraged. More rest, less swimming, and more Bex powders had been prescribed.

The effects of iron deficiency due to excessive menstrual blood loss or the heightened need for iron in the blood of female athletes was not yet a topic for discussion or medical attention in 1950s South Australia.

A couple of teammates entered the locker room.

"Oh, Henny, too bad," one said sympathetically. "You didn't make it. What happened? You just couldn't get going?"

I shrugged—a gesture learned from my mother at an early age—and walked to the showers. "The Olympics have just disappeared from my destiny," I told them.

"You don't know that. You've still got next year," a swimmer I liked and respected and who would make it to the Olympics said. "We all have our disappointing years."

When I left the showers, I found my mother waiting for me. She stood nearby as I dressed. "Are you alright?"

I shrugged again. There were no words.

She picked up my bag and we walked outside, where my dad and sister were waiting.

I looked at my dad. "I'm a loser." I fought back the tears.

"Oh really?" He grimaced. "It doesn't take much to turn you into a loser, then. So, with all the State Championships you have won, you are a loser?"

We walked to the car in silence.

"I couldn't make it on the national level," I muttered, slumping down in the backseat of the car. "I am not a winner, so that makes me a loser."

"Oh, stop it." My dad's voice rose to a level of impatience. "Are you telling me that all your friends who have been cheering you on all these years at every event but who never won any themselves are all losers?"

I didn't respond. So many swimmers in both clubs had stood at the end of the pool yelling my name in support and encouragement as I competed. How could they stand never being a winner? Why hadn't I thought about that before?

"I think I'll give up swimming," I said.

"Well, that certainly sounds like a loser to me," my dad said.

Seated in the backseat of the car, I could see him frowning at me in the rearview mirror. "So if you can't be first, you'll give up the sport? I guess you are just too important to cheer on your teammates who are faster than you?"

"Remember to give me your swimsuit," my mom chimed in. "If you are not going to swim anymore, maybe I'll wear it."

Neither of my parents had much patience for self-pity.

Tears prickled behind my eyes, and I sank back in silence in the seat, where Laura, who had been quiet all this time, grabbed my arm and leaned up close to comfort me. I loved my little sister.

When we arrived home, my mother put on the kettle, because as she said, "A cup of hot tea will make us all feel better."

I started to cry.

"Don't cry, Henny," Laura said, and I burst into sobs.

"I feel so ashamed. I let everyone down."

"Why feel ashamed?" my dad demanded. "You did the best you could." He looked in my eyes. "Listen to me. You are disappointed, of course. That's normal. But no need for shame. You did nothing wrong."

"And you are exhausted," my mother added. "Drink your tea, and let's get some sleep. We can talk tomorrow. Everything always looks better in the morning."

She made me smile through my tears. "For you," I said. "In the morning, I may feel worse."

"Maybe it's just a sign to ease up," my mother said as she hugged me good night.

Guided by her powerful intuition that she believed came from God, she'd always taught me there was a reason for the challenges we faced.

But a sign to ease up and do what?

My body had not felt up to the assigned task, I knew it. It had failed me—or had I failed it? I had always trusted my body and my mind to place me among the best, to make me a winner. How could I trust myself now?

Chapter 28
Where Is My Hat?
Adelaide, South Australia, 1955

In the winter months that followed, I struggled with my inner self-demeaning voice, my body, and my mother. What did it mean to be a winner or a loser?

If I was not strong like my mother, the fierce Resistance heroine who had been my rock and role model during those traumatic years in Nazi-occupied Amsterdam, then who was I?

My dad approached my dilemma in his usual philosophical manner.

"Have you ever thought that there are other ways to be a winner? Maybe a winner is someone who can support others," he challenged me. "It takes courage, strength, and a winning attitude to recognize that other swimmers are now faster than you. Maybe you can even embrace your own vulnerability? That's difficult and even frightening, I know."

I had no answer.

He added, "Sport should be for your enjoyment. If you don't enjoy it anymore, you shouldn't be swimming."

"But I do enjoy it," I argued. "You don't understand."

"Then enjoy it," he said, "and don't be so focused on winning."

My mother, meanwhile, had remained surprisingly silent. I sensed her disappointment that I had not placed in the National finals and that our Olympic dream may have just been dashed, but she had not said a word.

I guess her silence bothered me, because one evening, as I was drying the dishes, I told her, "I'm only seventeen. If I train hard, I could perhaps be ready for the 1960 Olympics.."

"Henny, maybe it's a good thing you didn't win," she said. "Swimming isn't all there is to life. All that intense butterfly stroke training creates huge arm and neck muscles. You are a pretty girl, but if you keep training harder and harder for another Olympics, you will look like a wrestler."

"A wrestler?" I couldn't believe what she was saying. "So what I am left with is how I look—that's all you think I am worth?" I snarled at her in disbelief. "If I keep training, I will never get a man to love me? Oh, sure, I will be secondhand goods like the doctor said. I'll be an old maid with a thick, ugly neck."

"No, I didn't—"

"You mean it!" I raised my voice. "You are happy I didn't make it."

"No." She shook her head. "I am just thinking that there may be another way of looking at your disappointment. Maybe winning at swimming isn't everything."

This from my mother? The athletic woman who had attended my every swim meet? The mother who I sometimes thought would tumble into the pool in her exuberant excitement to cheer me on when I was competing? The mother who demanded excellence and perfection from both her children?

"Maybe it's not your destiny," she said softly, almost to herself. "I have a feeling you are meant to do something else."

Her words frightened me. Was she telling me that all I had to fall back on was my appearance, the looks I'd inherited from her?

Over the years, my mother's intuition had always hit the right note. But my identity as a swimmer had given me a sense of control while I adapted to being a stranger in an alien land. I was in charge. I couldn't let her take that away from me.

I received more than my share of attention for my looks that winter. There were plenty of whistles when I walked down the street, invitations to dinners, movies, and dances from boys and even older and sometimes married men.

I chose to go out with the nice boys. Boys who mostly took the bus to come pick me up. Boys who only asked for a good night kiss as a reward when they dropped me off at the doorstep, where my dad would always coincidentally step out of the front door at that precise moment to hang the billycan on the porch for the next morning's milk truck delivery. He would stop, wave, look at his watch, and wave again, a token of approval that I had been delivered home at the promised time.

They were sweet boys who bought me chocolates and flowers and told me I was pretty. But who was I, really?

When I'd swum well, it was because I had spent hours swimming laps in training. When I'd done well in my studies at Lyceum or the correspondence school or business college, it was because I had honed and disciplined my mind with reading and homework assignments. When I could transcribe shorthand squiggles and type them up in well-crafted letters in English, the language in which I had become fluent, I felt I had achieved something. I liked my mind.

But how should I feel about my prettiness? I had done nothing to earn it.

Sometimes I hated it. It attracted uncomfortable comments or even attacks over which I had no control. I thought of the truckers and their lewd comments at the steel company, the boss who'd pinned me to the wall, and even the wandering hands of men groping for a "feel" on the crowded buses that my girlfriends and I took home after work.

No, being pretty did not make me feel strong, powerful, or accomplished. It made me feel vulnerable and at times like prey.

I had been so sure I knew the woman I was going to be—a woman like my mother, fierce and strong—but I didn't feel fierce or strong. I felt weak and confused.

The night after my troubling conversation with my mother, I had a dream that presented me with a new dilemma:

I am looking for a hat to wear. It's for an important occasion. I am standing in a cloakroom, and I am facing a row of shelves on which a variety of elegant women's hats are carefully displayed. The hats are arranged by different styles and colors. I search carefully for the hat that is mine, but I don't know what it looks like. And as I examine the hats one by one, I realize every single one of them belongs to my mother. They are all my mother's hats. Where is my hat? What does my hat even look like?

When I woke up, I obsessed over the question.

Did the dream provide a sign or direction? Did I even know what I would want my own hat to look like? How would it be different from any one of my mother's? I was fortunate to be athletic like my mother. Blessed to have inherited her good looks, as I was too often told. How was I me and not her? Perhaps I was as weak as she was strong?

My inner confusion and turmoil lingered, but soon the summer months were upon us and I was once again back in the pool.

Chapter 29
A Brave Little Boy
Adelaide, South Australia, 1955

"His legs just dangled. They were useless, but he kept swimming. He was so brave, so courageous! You should have seen him!" I stumbled over the words in my excitement to share my experience that day.

As usual, we were gathered at the end of the day in the large, sunny kitchen of our suburban home. My mom was busy preparing our evening meal while my dad, my sister, and I sat around the Formica table, discussing that day's topics of interest.

One such topic was polio, the dreaded, often paralyzing disease that had been sweeping Australia and the rest of the world for the past few years. Before the discovery of the Salk vaccine, many swimming pools had been closed from time to time because of fear of contagion. Over a thousand Australians had died of the virus, and young people who survived were often left with deformed or lifeless limbs.

Along with some other seasoned swimmers, I had been chosen to be part of a volunteer group that assisted young polio survivors in an experimental aquatic therapy treatment at the Henley pool. Today had been my first day in the program.

* *

Waiting in the pool in our swimsuits, it was difficult to tell the ages of the boys and girls being lifted into the water by their caregivers. To me, they looked to be about eight years old—a little younger than my sister. Their young faces showed the normal mix of playful apprehension of children that age, but something set them apart from most of their peers: The legs of these six brave little warriors hung lifeless. Though they had survived polio, the disease had left their limbs paralyzed. The hope was that exercising in the saltwater pool might help restore some mobility and allow their bodies to regain a feeling of strength and confidence.

My fellow swimmers and I were each assigned a child.

I was introduced to a dark-haired little guy named Mike. He had a determined, serious expression on his face.

I shook his hand. "Good to meet you, Mike. My name is Henny. I will be your swim instructor."

"I was already learning to swim before I got polio," he said.

I liked the note of defiance in his voice. "Good on ya," I said. "That means you can still swim, and you can show me."

He lay down in the water, and I put one hand under his abdomen and another under his dangling ankles. We were in the shallowest end of the pool.

"Is it alright if I hold you up for a bit?" I asked him.

He nodded his head yes and began to move his arms in a dog-paddle stroke, but the lack of feeling in his legs clearly frustrated him.

"I don't think I can swim anymore," he spluttered. "I can't kick my legs. I can't feel them." He swallowed water. We took a break for him to cough while he held on to the side of the pool.

"Let's concentrate on your arms," I suggested. "Do you know how to do a breaststroke with your arms?"

He nodded and tried—and we both laughed. He was an absolute

natural. His strong little arms lifted the top of his body out of the water. He breathed in and out with ease. I put my hand under his dangling legs, and he began to move in the water using his arms and shoulders in a breaststroke movement.

"Hey," I yelled as he moved into the deeper end of the pool, "slow down! I can't keep up with you."

"I still can't feel my legs." He grabbed my arms.

"You're a darn fish," I told him. "Fish don't need legs to swim. What kind of fish are you, anyway?"

"I'm a shark." He turned his head and tried the crawl this time.

"Hey, good on ya, mate," I said, laughing. "Nothing can stop a shark in the water."

I watched as he connected with the healthy parts of his body and pulled himself through the water, carried along by his small arms and young determination.

"Can I put my hand under your tummy to support you?" I asked.

He nodded yes, his face showing a resolve that made me smile. I had seen that look of purpose on the face of every competitive swimmer I'd ever met.

Oh, how I wanted him to swim. How I wished at that moment that I had the power to make those little legs move again.

I let him go on his own for a couple of strokes, knowing his caregiver was watching me carefully from the side of the pool. He did it: His legs were still dangling, but he was staying afloat on his own. Then I lifted his legs gently with one hand, and together we swam across the width of the pool.

Did his legs move a little on their own? I asked myself at one point. I was sure they had, but it was probably my hope and imagination.

I'm not sure what happened in that moment, exactly, but something in me grew up or woke up. With a flash of recognition, I suddenly knew in my bones what it meant to be a real champion. This little boy should be given a medal!

"You are a champion," I told him as we swam back to the other side of the pool.

I knew he could sense I meant it. Truth has a way of communicating honesty that penetrates depths far below verbal communication. As I stayed at his side, hands ready to lift his dangling ankles, he swam all the way to the steps on his own.

There, his caregiver took over from me.

"You're a winner," I told him as he was being lifted out of the pool to his wheelchair. "You deserve a medal."

His whole beautiful little face wrinkled up into a big, spontaneous grin.

"You should be so proud of yourself," I said.

With some prodding from his caregiver, he murmured a shy, "Thank you."

"No," I said, "thank you for letting me swim with you. You are a champion. Always remember that!"

He nodded. His infectious, triumphant grin filled me with a feeling of joy that lasted all day.

"He was so darn brave," I told my mom and dad that evening. "I wonder if he will ever walk again. I hope he will be okay."

"You can pray for him," my mother said.

"It sounds like he will be okay in his life; he is already a teacher," my dad said thoughtfully. "He taught you what a real champion, a real winner, looks like. Didn't he?"

"It felt wonderful to help him feel strong," I said. "It made me so happy."

My dad just smiled.

I liked the thought of little Mike being a teacher in his life. I also liked that I could pray for him, even if I wasn't sure how I felt about a God who let little children become paralyzed by a polio virus.

That partially paralyzed little boy gave me a hint that day of what I wanted to do in my life. I wanted to help people find their strength, the warrior within them.

I didn't yet have a clue what that would look like; that awareness would come many years later.

For now, I just felt grateful that I could feel my legs when I swam.

Chapter 30
The Americans
Adelaide, South Australian summer 1955-56

"Why is a pretty girl like you sitting all by herself?"

Two well-built, good-looking young men wearing big smiles and tiny swim trunks sat down on either side of me.

Their accents told me they were Americans.

I was sitting by myself on the bleachers on the side of the Adelaide City Pool, where the South Australian Amateur Swimming Association had over the past few days conducted an Olympic Preview event that included diving, water polo, and swimming exhibitions in aid of the Australian Olympic Swim Training Fund.

Most of the participants were enjoying a late afternoon gathering before returning to their homes in different states and even other countries. Young, healthy swimmers and divers splashed and laughed in the pool; others gathered on the side and in the bleachers, sharing autographs and addresses or arranging future meetings.

"Why the glum look?" asked the shorter American with the blond, wavy hair, whom I recognized as one of the outstanding divers sure to win a medal in the upcoming Olympics. "Name is Bob, by the way," he added.

"I know; I saw you dive." I liked his warm smile. "You're impressive."

As a state champion, I had been invited, along with some other five-dozen swimmers, to participate in a 55-yard exhibition swim. It felt strange to be included in an event that was meant to be a preview to the Olympics, and I fought the disappointment that lingered. The knowledge that my dream of being an Olympian had ended still saddened me.

I continued to swim in competitive events this season, and I would manage wins in both the state 220-yard individual medley and the 220-yard breaststroke. It had even looked for a moment like I might participate in the National Championships in Sydney, which doubled as a selection event for the Olympics—but in the end, I was just not fast enough.

It turned out, however, that disappointments and defeats could not stop me from diving into that pool every day and pushing myself as hard as I could. Swimming and competition were apparently in my blood—the love of swimming from my father, the competitiveness from my mother. But without the Olympic goal, I felt somewhat adrift, still struggling with a loss of identity. The image I carried with me of little Mike challenged any feelings of self-pity—he had shifted my view of what it meant to be a champion—but I still did not have a sense of who I was if I wasn't training in the pool for the next big event.

Since the great coach to the Olympians Harry Gallagher had taken over the management of the City Baths in Adelaide and brought the stars of Australian swimming with him from Sydney, the city pool now sported both resident and visiting Olympic swimmers who craved Harry's guidance.

It was both fun and exciting to be splashing about with Dawn Fraser, Margaret Gibson, Jon Henricks, and others who would soon win the gold for Australia in Melbourne. It had raised our competitive camaraderie to a new high. I'd even managed to beat Dawn in a surprise win in the 200-yard breaststroke one day. Of course, "Dawn was off her game" that day, according to the sports pages the next morning—and yes, she managed to beat me by a length the following week—but the friendly competitive atmosphere rekindled my enthusiasm, especially when Coach Gallagher put his hand on my shoulder and said, "Work on that kick and look to the 1960 Olympics."

"You are Henny de Vries. I saw you swim the breaststroke. Powerful stroke," said the taller lean American on my right. "Name is Jay."

"Not good enough to get me to the Olympics," I said with pretend haughtiness.

"So you and I are the non-Olympians." He laughed.

"Well, if you are not an Olympian, what are you doing here?" I challenged him.

"I like mingling with the Olympian gods and goddesses." He chuckled. Then, his eyes meeting mine with an intensity I had not expected, he said, "Isn't it the thrill of the sport itself? When I stand on the edge of that high-diving platform, looking down on that little aquamarine patch of water below me, I get a thrill of anticipation. It's not just about the medals."

I smiled inwardly. He sounded like my dad.

"Henny," Bob chimed in, "how can you not be a winner? You are Dutch! You're from Holland, right?'

I nodded. "Amsterdam."

"Ever been back?"

"No, but I intend to when I have saved up enough money." For the past two years, I had been saving a small amount of my earnings each week. My aim was to have enough money for a return airplane ticket to Amsterdam and the cost of the train from there to Rotterdam to see my friends, aunts, uncles, and cousins. I'd been promised free room and board in both cities. But I was a long way from achieving my goal.

"My father helped liberate the south of Holland at the end of WWII," Jay interrupted, his tone serious. "He loved the Dutch people."

"Without American soldiers like your dad, I probably wouldn't be alive." I surprised myself with my response, because I did not like to talk about the past. The future held the hope that mattered.

"You must have been a little girl in the war," Jay said. "Was your family impacted?"

I shrugged, not wanting to remember. "Yeah, but that was a long time ago."

To change the subject, I turned to Bob on my other side. "So, what places should I visit in America?"

He thought for a moment. "Coming from the flatlands of Holland, you should probably see the Rocky Mountains. They're spectacular. Visit Colorado."

I didn't know much about Colorado, except that it had snow-covered mountains and cowboys.

"You can't live there," I said. "You don't look like a cowboy."

He grinned. "No, don't care much for horses. My steed is a Ford convertible."

"Where do you live?" I turned to Jay.

"California."

Oh yes, I knew about California. The state where movies were created and Esther Williams, the celebrity actress of synchronized swimming whom I so admired, made her home.

"I definitely plan to see California one day," I said.

"If you visit the US, you'll have plenty of free places to stay," Bob said. "Our diving and swimming communities are friendly, and they would love to host a Dutch-Australian. You are just the right mix."

Jay brought his face closer to mine. "Yes, Dutch-Australian with an Olympian goddess smile."

I found myself laughing at their brash American mannerisms. And thrilled with their suggestion that being Dutch-Australian was "the right mix" and not an immigrant fault line between two parts of me, a past and present, that had to compete for recognition.

The Americans and I chatted some more about my desire to travel and see the world. They painted a picture of golden beaches in California, skyscrapers in New York City, and mountains in Colorado, where apparently everyone lived happily ever after.

"You make America sound like a mystical land where you can shapeshift yourself into whatever or whoever you want to be," I said.

They both laughed. "It is. It is."

"That's what Australians told us when they seduced my parents into coming to Australia."

"Well, you must come see for yourself," Jay said in a way that made me blush.

His sparkling eyes held me captive; his naked thigh pressed against mine. He turned his muscular chest too close and put his hand on my arm, and I wondered what it would feel like to have him put both arms around me and kiss me.

The thought caught me off guard. The heat between my thighs spread up my torso. I knew my neck and face were turning a telltale purple red.

"The sun's too hot." I jumped up and dove into the pool to cool off.

I swam a hard, fast freestyle length, but my thoughts and images were not on an Olympic gold medal but on being held by a young man's athletic body, our mouths seeking one another's as we splashed in the waves off the beach of California; on our bare skin touching as we dried off in the sand; on us driving off in a convertible holding hands, the wind in our hair.

Hadn't my mother said that "intentions are like prayers sent into the universe that come back as destiny"?

Her words rang in my ears as I climbed out of the pool and said goodbye to my new American friends.

"Maybe we'll see you in America," Bob said, and he and Jay laughed.

Maybe, I thought.

As I grew older, I would often look back on the way destiny grants us glimpses of what lies ahead. In those moments, I would feel as if my life were being choreographed by a power infinitely greater and more mysterious than my own willful determination.

Chapter 31
Serendipity or Destiny?
Adelaide, South Australia, 1956

"Henny, you need to get up. It's midmorning. You are wasting the weekend." My mother's cheerful voice pierced the maudlin lethargy that held me immobilized in my bed.

I pulled the blankets up over my head. "Just go away," I muttered, wanting to scream.

Didn't she realize there was no reason to get up? The pools had been closed for the Australian winter months. Olympians were training in other states for the Games in November. I would be a spectator only. And I hated my job.

I tried to fight the feelings of uselessness that had plagued me since the pools closed, feelings that at times threatened to overwhelm me.

My mind craved stimulation. I had begun to look around for a new job but so far had not found anything that matched my skills. The bosses at the joinery were friendly and paid me a good salary, but the typing of invoices and the limited demand on my secretarial skills just did not challenge my imagination. I was bored to death. All my dreams had vaporized into thin air.

Many days, I would just lie on my bed and feel the tears well up as feelings of being a loser took hold of my mind and would not let go. Not only would I not be an Olympic swimmer, but I also would never be a journalist.

How many times had I told my parents and friends about my dream to work at a newspaper? But gradually, the dream had faded into a fantasy. Hadn't I been told often enough that girls didn't have careers in 1950s Australia? Didn't I realize that we were meant to become mothers and run the households for husbands, the men who attained the careers we dreamed of?

Besides, I lacked the necessary education. In most major newspapers, a young person hoping for a career in Australian journalism was expected to have a leaving certificate before starting an internship. In the British Commonwealth, the leaving certificate was awarded to students sixteen years or older who had completed the necessary secondary or high school courses and passed a special examination. And, of course, I had not completed the necessary secondary high school courses. *If only I had not been so stubborn and insisted on business college instead of going back to finish my high school courses,* I scolded myself daily.

To escape the darkness of my negative inner narrative, I had continued to swim in the ocean after the pools were closed, before the water just got too cold. But one day, as I swam a long distance out, I'd wondered what it would be like to just keep swimming and never come back. Could I swim to Amsterdam—to America? Or just keep swimming till I was too tired to swim back; just sink to the bottom of the ocean like a mermaid?

I had swum back to the shore that day, but the thought lingered. If I could just keep swimming, maybe I would feel better.

"Henny." My mother entered my bedroom again. "Get up. You can't just lie in bed all day."

My eyes watered up with tears. "Don't you understand? I have no reason to get up. I don't have anywhere to go. Just leave me alone."

"No, I won't let you waste a lovely day and lie there feeling sorry for yourself. You need to get up and get dressed," she said in her no-nonsense voice.

"All right, I will, and then I'm leaving. I need to get out of here." I uttered the words more to myself than to her.

As I started to get dressed, I remembered that when we'd left the Netherlands for Australia, I had been assigned my own passport. My father had always kept it with his and my mother's, insisting that passports needed to be kept in a "safe place."

I turned to my mother. "Where did Daddy put my passport?"

"Why do you want your passport?"

"Why? Because I want to leave. I cannot live here anymore. I'm an adult, and I can't have you tell me who I am and what to do," I yelled. I pulled the dress over my head, slipped on my shoes, and ran out of the house, slamming the door behind me.

I heard the door reopen. "Stop this nonsense right now!" My father's words came at me, loud and stern. I knew he meant business. He followed me down the front path and grabbed my arm. Turning me around so I faced him, he said, "You come inside and stop this drama!"

I tried to jerk away from him. "You need to give me my passport. I can work, I can be on my own."

My dad kept his grip on my arm. "If you leave, I will call the police. I will not let you be a silly runaway girl who puts herself in danger. You are smarter than that."

The police? Was he crazy? But I knew he meant to stop me.

He led me into the house, pushed me down onto a chair at the kitchen table, and handed me a glass of water.

"Now," he said, "we are going to talk. What's going on with you?

You are intelligent, pretty, a state swimming champion. You have wonderful friends, live in a comfortable home. What is going on?"

The tears inside me turned into wild sobs that turned into coughing fits and wet my face, neck, and dress. "I don't know."

"It's okay." He got up and poured me a small glass of the port wine that he and my mom occasionally liked to sip after dinner. "Sip this. Slowly. This drama doesn't solve anything."

"I feel like a nothing; I have nothing to look forward to," I sobbed. "I am sick of typing invoices every day."

"Then it sounds like you really do need another job," my dad said.

"And maybe see some of your friends," my mother added as she sat on a chair on the other side of my dad. "You have been lonely since the pools closed."

I nodded. My watering eyes blurred their faces, but I could hear the concern in their voices.

"I tried to be strong," I whispered, "but I don't know how. I can't see my dreams anymore."

"You need to see your friends and find another job. It will happen," my mother said, always confident. "God will help you."

I wasn't so sure of that, but it helped to hear her say it.

"But remember," my dad said after I had stopped crying and calmed down, "drama and running away solve nothing."

"There are always solutions," my practical mother, with her unshakable faith and determination, added. She put her hand on mine. It felt warm and reassuring.

I had always depended on her strength and intuition—when I was a terrified little girl and the Nazis broke into our house to take my Jewish foster sister in Amsterdam; in the months when we almost died of starvation before the war ended. She had been my rock before we immigrated to Australia. But something had changed since we'd moved here. Her difficulty learning the language, her dependence on me to be her translator, made me feel as if I were the parent at times. Especially in interactions when people could not understand her and turned to me to ask what she meant to say. Her constant references to me being her "brave girl" in the war felt manipulative, as if she needed to keep me little so she could appear strong again.

But she was strong. I knew that deep inside of me. It hit me in that moment that there was no doubt in my mind that in a crisis, she would always be there. She would be my rock, and perhaps my need for that did not make me a weak little girl, even though it felt that way and scared me sometimes.

I looked at her and whispered, "Thank you."

She nodded and patted my hand.

Feeling a little more hopeful, I resumed my regular routine of skipping rope that night. It was an integral part of my winter exercise when the pools were closed. I usually skipped outside for an hour or so after work. I would look up and make up stories in my head about faraway civilizations on the many stars that twinkled in the sky, then I would see the Southern Cross and feel the magic of living in the Southern Hemisphere.

But that night, after I picked up the rope and went outside, I looked at the stars and wondered: Was there really a God who choreographed our lives, as my mother seemed to believe—a divine energy that cared—or did we just exist in a mysterious world of infinite, unanswered questions that held the secrets to our fate, as my father liked to say?

Dot and Jane were already seated when I arrived, but they jumped up to hug me when I walked up.

In the days following the pep talk from my parents, at my mother's insistence, I'd contacted Dot, Jane, and Helen. It had taken some speedy letter exchanges, since a couple of us did not have telephones at home, but we'd managed to arrange this lunch at a small new restaurant on Rundle Street.

"You're looking great," we all told one another and caught up with smiles on recent happenings in our lives.

But after about twenty minutes, we began to wonder what had happened to Helen.

"She is usually the more punctual one among us," we agreed in shared concern.

"There she is." Dot pointed. "Hey, who is that good-looking bloke with her?"

Helen sat down on the chair that the young man who accompanied her pulled out for her before sitting next to her. We gaped. He was gorgeous.

"Sorry I'm late," she said with her usual disarming smile. "I had to wait for this lovely man to finish work. Let me introduce you to my new friend Dan."

A dark-haired young man with high cheekbones and the gentlest eyes I had ever seen in such a strong male face, Dan held out his hand to each of us, repeated our names, and sat back while we gazed adoringly at him.

Helen smiled as she turned to me. "Henny, do you still want to work at a newspaper?"

"Yes." I hesitated. What was she doing?

"Well, Dan is a reporter at *The Advertiser.*"

He nodded. "Helen tells me you're looking for a job and you have secretarial experience."

I just stared. My mind went blank.

"The chief of staff at *The Advertiser* is looking for a new secretary. I could recommend you for an interview if you like."

Could this be happening? I didn't know what to say without gushing or babbling some inane response. My mind would not let me access any intelligent words. As if in a hypnotic trance, I just sat in numbed silence as this friendly, good-looking young journalist continued to address me.

"It's a secretarial position, but you would be an integral member of the Editorial Department, taking dictation from the chiefs of staff, lots of interaction with the journalists in the newsroom. You'd be sharing an office with another secretary, Pauline. She is great, very experienced. I am sure you'd like her."

Did I answer him? I would never remember.

"The hours are a bit strange," he added.

"Job interview? Secretary to the chief of staff?" I finally managed to speak, but all I could do was repeat phrases he'd said back to him.

Helen looked immensely pleased with herself. "Maybe you can stop growing fins, Henny, and live a life."

Two days later, I walked up the well-worn steps of the old three-story building on the corner of King William Street that was home to Adelaide's morning newspaper. Butterflies did a crazy flutter dance in my nervous stomach as I found my way to the office of the chief of staff of the Editorial Department.

A tall, handsome man with a gentle British demeanor held out his hand. "Alan Williams. You must be Miss de Vries."

I returned his warm handshake, liking him immediately.

"You're here to apply for the secretarial position, I see," he said. "Well, I hope you type as fast as you swim." I must have looked taken aback, because he smiled. "Your fame as a state swimming champion did catch our attention. We are a newspaper."

My face flushed as I responded, "Yes, I am a fast typist, and my references will show that I have very good secretarial skills." In the quiet moment that followed, I added, "And I've always dreamed of working for a newspaper."

"Well, maybe you'll get your wish," he said kindly. "Let's give your skills a small test, shall we?"

He handed me a notebook and dictated a practice letter to the governor at Government House that announced the day's news headlines. After typing it up and handing it to him, I answered a couple more questions pertaining to my educational background and secretarial experience.

I left the office feeling strangely optimistic—and not many hours later, that same day, I received the news that I had been hired.

Yes, I would be working at the prestigious Adelaide morning newspaper.

Maybe my mother was right, and intentions really were like prayers that could make dreams come true.

Chapter 32
My Own Hat
Adelaide, South Australia, 1956

Was I ready? I stood still, looked up at the old newspaper building in front of me, and, as if about to dive into a swimming pool for an important race, took a deep, deep breath. My first day on the job at the Adelaide *Advertiser*, South Australia's largest morning newspaper.

"It's your destiny," my mother had said when I was putting on a conservative skirt and blouse in readiness for this new phase of my life.

As anticipation mixed with my nervousness and excitement, I wondered if she was right.

I entered the front hall and made my way to the office of the chief of staff's secretaries. The aging edifice embraced me with a myriad of sensations. Its darkened old woodwork, its smells of ink and paper mixed with cigarette smoke, and the sounds of clickety-clack typewriters and ringing telephones alerted me that I had just entered a new and unfamiliar world.

"Well, here you are," Mr. Williams greeted me with a warm smile. "I want to introduce you to Mr. Doug Jervis; he is in charge when I am not here."

An energetic-looking man sporting an appealing, boyish grin shook my hand. "Welcome to our editorial family; I'm sure you will be happy here."

His friendly welcome calmed my nervousness.

"I'm afraid we are going to have to start you off right away," Mr. Williams said. "I think you already know that this is your desk." He pointed to the desk facing the entrance door. "Miss Rice"—I assumed he was referring to Pauline—"will be here this afternoon to familiarize you more, but right now I need you to take a couple of letters that must be sent off this morning. You think you are ready for that?"

"Yes, sir." I picked up the steno pad from the desk and followed him through the adjoining door into his office.

I spent the remainder of the morning transcribing and typing up the Pitman characters on my notepad as I tried to remember the correct punctuation rules. When I handed the typed-up letters, along with their carbon copies, to Mr. Williams, he smiled his kind smile and said, "Very good, but perhaps you do not need to be so generous with your commas. Might a little review be in order?"

I felt my face redden.

My year at the joinery, where most of my work had consisted of typing up invoices, had not helped me retain the English rules of punctuation, especially the use of commas, which I definitely needed to review. My considerate new boss was right, and I was grateful for his very kind delivery.

"I'm sorry, sir, I will," I said, and I hastened back to my desk.

When it was time for lunch, I marched to the nearest bookstore to buy the most recent copy of a book on English grammar and punctuation. Upon my return, Pauline had already arrived and was seated at her desk. Tall and attractive, a couple of years my senior, she greeted me with a big, welcoming smile. She radiated confidence, and I hoped we could become friends and she would be my guide in the months ahead. We each had our own desk and would take turns working the two shifts: 9:00 a.m. to 5:00 p.m. and 2:00 p.m. to 9:00 p.m.

Our spacious office faced the street through large, almost floor-to-ceiling windows and sat adjacent to the office of the chief of staff. Both offices opened onto the newsroom on the other side, where rows of male writers with inquisitive, creative minds and fast fingers generated a rapid clickety-clack clatter from their upright typewriters.

Pauline introduced me to the reporters in the newsroom of the Editorial Department and gave me a tour of some of the other newspaper sections in the building. There were different offices for the sports pages, agricultural news, and arts and social pages, and as she took me to meet various editors and reporters, I noticed that only the editor of the social pages was a woman. The newspaper world was clearly a realm that was ruled by the men.

I was not surprised, and while it registered, I did not think too much more about it at the time. I was too overwhelmed, excited, and determined to establish my own place to think any more deeply on it. From the predictable boundaries of the swimming pool, with its familiar black line down the middle of the lane to guide the miles I swam each day, I had stepped into the bustling, chaotic world of writers and reporters of news events, editorial opinions, commentaries, and human-interest stories.

I thought I knew all about competition, but in the days and weeks ahead, I quickly learned that competition in the world of swimming and competition in the newspaper world bore no resemblance to each other. I could not begin to compare the demands placed on a competitive swimmer, with mind, muscle, and every movement exacting total attention and excellence from their body, to the intellectual, creative, and emotional demands and frenzy of the newsroom competition that I now witnessed.

The mental and creative battle for the perfect story, for the byline that showed one's name above an article. The meticulous fact-checking that validated the who, what, when, and where of an event. The push to be the first to cover an incident, to choose the words that created that particularly unique focus that would elicit in a reader an emotional and intellectual response, or to give an occurrence the slant and emphasis that would please and satisfy an editor. The creative complexity and demand placed on the writers competing to generate the best story of that day. All of it boggled and thrilled my mind.

But I also discovered that the camaraderie I'd experienced with other competitive swimmers, which included a focus on the utmost health, discipline, and well-being of the physical body, had left me woefully unprepared for the often hard-drinking and heavy-smoking worldliness of the male-dominated newsroom, where, in reference to my developed bosom and state breaststroke swimming championships, the joke circulated as to who among them would be the new "breaststroke" champion.

It bothered me. I didn't like it, but I didn't quite know how to deal with it.

Despite the jokes, most of the men made me feel like I was among friends from the day I started. But one afternoon, one of the older journalists—a large, married man—stepped in front of me and faced me as I walked across the newsroom.

"Hey, Miss Deep Freeze." He chortled at his own distorted pronunciation of my last name. "How about you and I go out for a romantic dinner this evening?"

Shocked and surprised, I blurted out in a loud, angry voice, "That's not my name, and you are married!"

My response elicited raucous laughter from the men in the room. Confused and ashamed, my face hot and flushed, I ran back into my office and asked Pauline, "Why do they think it's so funny?"

"Oh, you are so naive." She shook her head; she had been at the job for a while and had a sophisticated familiarity with the newsroom environment. "Look, they're great guys, for the most part, but they are men." She laughed.

Then she took me under her wing—taught me who was trustworthy, who liked to tease, who was on the make, and who to watch out for.

I started to ponder the whole naivete thing. Hadn't Helen also laughed at our naivete when we met with Dot and Jane?

I went to find Dan, Helen's friend who'd gotten me my new job. He often checked in with me with a warm, "How're you doing, Henny? Adjusting?" And I would thank him again and tell him how much I loved being amid all the news and stories.

"Dan, do you think I am naive?" I demanded.

Clearly taken aback by my question, he smiled and said, "Oh, maybe that's something you should ask Helen."

"No," I said firmly, "she's already told me she thinks I am naive, and so does Pauline. And it has all to do with my relationships with men, so I want to hear it from a man. And I trust you. Or maybe that's naive, too."

"What brought on this question?" Dan asked seriously.

"Well, we all work together, right? It's a friendly atmosphere, but why do some of you still make comments, leer, or whistle when I walk through the newsroom? Why the awful breaststroke jokes?"

"Wow, not easy questions," Dan said. "No easy answers. We're just dumb blokes, I guess. Nothing personal. It's just men!"

"I know you are men, but am I naive if it surprises and bothers me?"

Dan was silent for a moment, then said, "I think you are just very innocent. Didn't the guys you swim with ever come on to you? My God, you are all almost completely naked together."

It made me laugh, because it was true, and I had personally enjoyed some of those almost-naked hugs. "Well, we hug, sometimes kiss, we flirt, of course—I suppose some may go all the way—but I feel safe with them. I just haven't experienced any meanness. The way some of the men in the newsroom tease feels so predatory. Competitive swimmers need to take care of our bodies. We can't drink or smoke. Is that being innocent?"

"I'd call it wholesome," Dan said. "But you can be a bit confusing. You have a sexy walk and a come-hither smile, but you are also a good girl. I think it drives some of the guys in the newsroom crazy. You walk across that room and they see a wench, but you think they see a good girl."

He looked away. "To put it crassly, they want you to know they'd like to get in your panties. And I guess you are naive if you don't recognize that."

"Is that all men ever want?" I asked, feeling a little angry. *Why did I even bring up the question?*

Dan laughed. "You really should talk with Helen."

"No, you are a man. I want you to tell me. I know Helen is not naive. I guess you would say she is definitely not innocent, wouldn't you?"

"No." He smiled. "She knows the ropes. She's pretty savvy!"

"So, you like savvy girls who are not naive?" I was determined to get to the bottom of this.

"Well, I know where I stand with her, because she knows what she wants and she lets me know."

"You mean, she knows that men just want to go all the way—get in her panties, as you say."

He looked at me. "They may want to, but that doesn't mean they do. Look, most of the guys in the newsroom are incredible journalists and are in relationships they care about. They're just human, Henny."

I shook my head. "No, they're men."

At that we both laughed.

"See," he said, "that's the wench talking, not the naive girl."

Still feeling some angry confusion, I asked him, "Do you ever want to get in my panties?"

Looking horrified, Dan roared. "Hell no. Especially after this conversation; I feel like I'm your older brother."

I believed him, but I wondered if that meant I was still being naive.

Pauline and I soon worked out a routine for our alternate shifts. Not being an early morning person, I especially enjoyed the late evening shift. It often came with weird phone calls to our Editorial Department from insomniacs who swore they were being chased by aliens or had some sort of wild conspiracy story that they wanted the newspaper to publish. When the person who normally took those calls was not available, we routed the calls to one of the reporters on duty. Deciding which one to saddle with an especially persistent annoying or weirdo caller always elicited a chuckle.

I quickly discovered that I loved the bustle of different opinions, deadlines, news stories, and commentaries.

One day, I arrived for my morning shift to find the newsroom in uproar. Several of the journalists appeared to be engaged in a verbal battle over a particular news event.

"It's a story about suffering," one exclaimed loudly. "It needs my human-interest touch."

"It's political!" his opponent yelled. "The readers deserve the facts, not your opinions and weepy feelings."

A third added something about the need to focus on the paper's editorial position, at which point Mr. Williams walked in and settled the dispute by assigning the article to the man of his choosing—whereupon everyone went back to their respective desks to write the best possible article or story they could.

Despite the occasional heated argument, those same writers got together for a cold beer or two at the end of the day. In their presence, I came to enjoy and respect the wide range of creative personalities of the hardworking journalists who devote their lives to giving us the news each day. They helped me discover and recollect parts of myself that I would continue to develop and own in the years ahead. As I carried out my secretarial duties and absorbed the world of the Fourth Estate, my mind began to explode with ideas and intentions. I decided that I would travel the world, learn other languages, and write stories. I would find a way to study. I felt as if I was intending my destiny.

I began to dream about my fierce maternal grandmother, who thought women should write and study. I remembered how she never had the opportunity to write her stories and how proud she had been of me when I spoke my first French words in an elementary school play in Amsterdam. Some days I even felt as if her spirit inhabited me.

On a particular afternoon after work, I decided to walk over to the department store on Rundle Street and have a look around in the women's hats department.

"How may I help you?" an attractive female assistant wearing a dark blue cloche hat that sported a big yellow sunflower asked me.

"I am looking for a hat for myself," I said, trying to sound confident.

"Oh, I think this style would be perfect on you with your features and high cheekbones." She showed me a tan-colored, wide-brimmed, fedora-type hat.

I gasped. No! No! It was almost an exact duplicate of the hat my mother had worn when I was a little girl. She'd always told me it was her favorite.

"No, no, no, I don't want a brimmed hat," I protested, my voice raised so loud that I think I scared the poor girl.

Taking a step backward, she suggested softly, "Perhaps a cloche, like the one I am wearing?" She led me to a colorful display of a variety of cloche hats covered in flowers or bows.

"No—they are pretty," I tried to make my tone of voice gentler, "but they are not really what I have in mind."

What did I have in mind? What did my hat look like? Did it even exist?

Then I spotted them. On a side shelf, shoved aside like a litter of abandoned kittens, they lay in a bunched-up heap: French felt berets in every assortment of color.

I picked up a wrinkled black one, smoothed it out, put it on, and looked in the mirror. *Yes, yes! I'd found my hat!*

"Oh, it's you." The sales assistant smiled.

I didn't know if she meant it or if she simply saw a sale, but I didn't care. I had found my hat, a jaunty French beret.

I knew my grandmother, my Oma, was smiling—and of course, my mother had never owned and, I knew for sure, would never wear a black beret.

When the swimming pools opened again at the beginning of the Australian spring months, I jumped into the chilly water and swam a hundred hard laps to calm my intoxicated mind—and I continued to do so whenever I was able to in the weeks that followed. I even managed to finally master that darn dolphin butterfly kick.

As I was leaving the *Advertiser* building on my way to the pool on one of those days, a male voice called out, "Henny de Vries!"

I turned around but did not recognize the tall young man, probably in his early twenties, with strawberry blond hair, a freckled face, and a booming voice.

"I saw you swim in the Swim Through Adelaide," he told me. "You swam the breaststroke. You'd never get me in that river." He held out his hand. "I'm Murray. I cover the local sports events."

We decided to walk together and ended up discussing the importance of sports in Australia and the peculiarities of being Westerners living in the Southern Hemisphere.

"I like the way Australia promotes and embraces sports," I said.

"Yes, we Aussies even upended the hallowed date of the Olympic Games!" He laughed.

It was a fact that the Summer Olympics had always been held in the July-August summer months of the countries in the Northern Hemisphere that hosted them. But this year, for the first time in Olympic history, the Games were to take place in Australia—and since July and August happened to be midwinter months Down Under, the 1956 Melbourne Olympiad was to be held at the beginning of Australia's summer, from November 22 to December 8.

"Who will you cheer for, the Dutch or the Aussies?" Murray asked.

"The Australians, of course," I said. "After all, they are my friends now, my teammates."

I did not share that a part of me felt disloyal even telling him that. After all, I was still Dutch, and I had swum with girls like me in Amsterdam when we all had dreams of becoming champions; I had an inner fault line that sometimes split me in two. But I made myself remember what the Americans had said about being a Dutch-Aussie: It was "the right mix."

"Maybe I'll cheer for the Dutch if they are so fast that they can actually beat the Aussies," I said.

Murray shook his head. "No, you have to choose."

Like choosing which queen you must honor, I thought to myself, but did not say anything.

"Will you be going to Melbourne to watch the Games?" he asked.

"I bought tickets for several of the swim events, but there is so much to learn in my new job, I don't think I want to take the time away," I said.

"If you want to sell them, I have some friends who might buy them for a reduced price," he said.

"That sounds good. Let me think about it, and I'll bring them to your office if I decide not to go."

"I'll do the haggling," he joked.

"And maybe I won't have to split myself in half and choose which country to cheer for," I said.

As it turned out, I wouldn't have a chance to test my loyalties: By November, we would hear the news that the Netherlands had decided to boycott the Olympic Games in a show of support for a people's uprising in Hungary that had been brutally crushed by the Russians that year. Along with Spain and several other countries, the Netherlands demonstrated their opposition to Russia's participation in the Games by not attending.

In my personal life, meanwhile, my emotional center of gravity would begin to shift away from my meditative lap swimming in the pool and toward the excitement and stimulation of the newspaper world and the stories we generated and inhabited. And I would soon wear my beret to the naturalization ceremony where I would become a bona fide Aussie.

Chapter 33
The Mississippi Steamboat Gambler and His Moll
Adelaide, South Australia, 1957

"I'll give you the shillings you need to stay in the game if you'll be my date for the Journalists' Ball," a male voice over my right shoulder whispered in my ear as I pushed back my chair.

It was a Friday evening, and a group of us from the newspaper had gathered for a party at a reporter's home. I had joined a game of poker that involved betting shillings and pennies. It appeared I was not very good at the card game, and after losing four shillings, I'd decided I was done. I needed my remaining shillings for the bus ride home.

I turned around to look at the skinny, dark-haired young man with glasses, not much older than me, who'd made the offer to keep me in the game. It was Pat, our editorial cartoonist. I had seen him around the newspaper a few times, but since he worked on a different floor and not in the newsroom, I had not paid much attention to him before.

"The Journalists' Ball is not for months," I said.

"Making sure I'm at the front of the line." He grinned. "It'll be fun."

Wow, he's full of himself, I thought, feeling a little annoyed. Does he think I'm for sale? "I don't need your shillings," I said. "I am going home." I stood up.

"I can drive you home." He pulled himself up to his full six-foot height and stepped in front of me with a big smile on his face.

"You have a car?" It was getting late, and I did not look forward to either the walk to the bus stop in the dark or the bus ride home. It might be nice to be chauffeured.

"Yup." He grinned again.

His pushy confidence annoyed but also intrigued me a little.

The intrigue would prove to be my undoing.

Driving me home, Pat shared that he needed a car because he lived with his family in Aldgate, in the Adelaide Hills.

"That must be a nice place to live," I said. "My dad likes to take us for drives up there on weekends now and then. You have some spectacular views of the sea from up there."

"It's alright," he said.

Since that subject didn't seem to interest him, I pursued a different one. "How did you come to be an editorial cartoonist?"

He told me it had been a serendipitous process. "I've always been an artist," he said, "drawn pictures since I was a little kid. One day I tried cartoons. The newspaper needed a cartoonist." He made it sound natural.

"Two of my uncles in Holland, my mother's brothers, are artists," I said. "I think they mostly paint landscapes. Do you still draw and paint also?"

"Sure," he said. "I think an artist should experiment with different subjects and approaches. But I intend to be famous one day."

"As an artist?" I asked.

"No, a political cartoonist. World famous!"

Boy, he sure is full of self-importance, I thought, a little taken aback.

"My mother says that intentions are like prayers that return as your destiny. If you pay attention," I offered.

"I believe that, too," he said.

The serious, thoughtful tone of his voice made me like him a little bit better.

We talked a little about the annual Journalists' Ball. Neither of us had ever attended it before. It would be a costume ball, and my arrogant cartoonist driver already had it all planned out.

"We can dress up as a Mississippi steamboat gambler and his sexy moll," he said.

"What's a moll?" I asked, unfamiliar with the term.

He laughed. "A gambler's girlfriend. I know where we can rent the costumes—I've already checked it out. I'll take you there."

I couldn't believe what I was hearing. Who was this cocky, skinny boy? He was not my type at all. I was attracted to men with athletic bodies—swimmers.

"In the meantime, we can go see a movie," he said as we pulled up to my house. "You can choose which one."

I hesitated. "I'm not sure."

"You can tell me at work tomorrow," he said cheerfully before stepping out of the car to open the door for me.

I wasn't sure how I felt about any of this as I watched him drive off.

The next day at work, he walked up to my desk.

"Have you thought about the movie?" he asked, as if I had already agreed to go. "I want to see the Disney animation film *Lady and the Tramp*," he said without waiting for my answer. "Walt Disney is a genius with his animation. I'd like to study his techniques."

It so happened that I too wanted to see that movie. I decided it couldn't hurt to go out with him again, since we were meeting to try out our costumes for the dance anyway.

"Okay," I agreed. "How about next weekend?"

Pat and I both thoroughly enjoyed the movie. I shrugged off his arm when he tried to put it around my shoulders midfilm, but I agreed to go out for "a cool drink or something" afterward.

In the busy milk bar close by, we shared how much we loved the animated antics and cute canine romance between Tramp, the mutt with street smarts who was a wizard at escaping the dogcatcher, and Lady, the pampered cocker spaniel whom Tramp affectionately nicknamed Pidge, after a pigeon, because of her naivety.

"I like the way *Lady and the Tramp* recaptures in such a fun way that old theme of love triumphing over seemingly insurmountable differences, like in *Beauty and the Beast*," I said. "It's clever."

"Who can resist a cocker spaniel and a mongrel mutt romance?" Pat quipped.

We both laughed.

"Yes, it's an age-old theme," Pat added. "It's even us—you're the beauty, you're Lady, and I'm the Tramp. And you know what?"

"What?" I asked. *Where was he going with this?*

"From now on, I'm calling you Pidge. I'm the Tramp, and you are Pidge."

"What, because I'm naive like a pigeon, like Lady in the movie?" I couldn't believe I was being called naive again. Really, who did he think he was, anyway—and why did I not feel more annoyed? "So, you have the street smarts," I teased him back. "You are the mutt, the mongrel, and I am the naive pigeon?"

"No, no, because you are beautiful—but I can't call you Lady. You are Pidge, and I'm your Tramp. Beauty and the Beast." He laughed.

"I thought you were my steamboat gambler and I was your moll." I found myself chuckling too, and I realized I was having fun joking around with this skinny boy who was not my type.

He took me to the costume shop a few days later. We tried on our costumes and practiced the roles of riverboat gambler, the rogue, and his sexy moll, ever the wench. I liked his playfulness and the way we could fantasize about ourselves in our different roles. He called me Pidge, just as he'd said he would, and I realized with a shock that I was looking forward to the night of the dance.

My mother was not too sure when I shared that I planned to attend the Journalists' Ball dressed in a skintight, black-sequined dress with one side slit up all the way to reveal a shapely leg. I also intended to hold a long cigarette holder in my hand, enhance my gray eyes with turquoise eyeshadow and black mascara, and wear a bright red lipstick, and my auburn hair would be dusted platinum and piled up on top of my head for the evening.

Yup, a gambler's moll. I liked it.

"Who is this boy?" she demanded. "Why do you have to look like a prostitute at the ball? We should meet him first."

As a little girl in Holland, I'd loved to dress up. When I was eleven years old, I had even asked my mom if I could take acting lessons. She had refused, saying I was a top student and she wanted me to focus on my studies. I suspected in later years that actresses were not held in high regard in her days.

"Oh, for gosh sakes," I cried. "I am eighteen, and there is nothing wrong with having fun and dressing up as a gambler's girlfriend. It's a Journalists' Ball!"

I used the word "girlfriend" rather than "moll" out of necessity;

my mother and I still communicated in Dutch, and sometimes it just took too much work to find the right translation for words.

On the night of the dance, at once nervous and excited, I took hours to powder and pile up my hair, make up my face, and get my dress and stockings just right.

My date arrived at the exact time promised. My heart skipped a beat when I saw him. He looked wickedly handsome with his thin moustache, black hat, and gambler's tie.

Sporting a cheeky grin, he took one look at me and whistled.

"So, you are the Mississippi steamboat gambler." My dad laughed and held out his hand. "You kids have fun. But get Henny home safely."

"Yes, boss," my date responded with a cocky shake of his head.

From that day on, my dad would always be "boss" to him.

My mother stepped toward him and leaned in so her face was close to his. "You'd better take good care of Henny," she said in her serious, no-nonsense tone of voice.

"I promise," he responded in an equally serious voice.

He held my hand as we walked out the door.

The Journalists' Ball swept me up into a magical night of dance, music, pleasure, and fantasy. Pat and I embodied the gambler and his moll, and we danced the night away. Photographed and lavishly praised for our costumes, our picture even appeared in the September/October issue of the *Advertiser Pi,* the in-house magazine that chronicled major events and happenings worth mentioning in the lives of the newspaper's personnel.

Pat began to drive me home after work, and one night after I finished the late shift, he took me to Luigi's—a small basement nightclub where coffee cups held nightcaps after hours and the dimly lit room throbbed with Eartha Kitt's sultry voice.

Our bodies sank into a velvet couch next to a low table, and as we sipped our drinks, we shared family history, hopes, and dreams. Pat understood the ancestral and nomadic restlessness that claims those of us who are one, two, or even three generations removed from our native lands. His father's family had come from Scotland.

"I plan to visit Fleet Street one day, spend time in London," he said.

"I plan to see Amsterdam again, visit my uncles, aunts, cousins, and friends in Holland," I said.

"My mother is an immigrant like you," he said. "She was born in London. Came to Australia with her parents when she was a little girl."

"Well, at least she had the right queen," I said.

He looked puzzled. I told him about being admonished by the teacher in the Bathurst Migrant Camp school, told to denounce my Dutch queen. "According to him, if I want to be an Aussie, I can only have one queen—the British one."

Pat roared with laughter. "Well, I think you should bloody well have two queens!"

I liked that.

"I want to see Paris and California," I said.

"New York," he said. "And newspapers all over the world."

"You are restless," I said.

"You are too," he said.

We leaned into each other. He put his hand on my thigh. He gave me my first cigarette. I felt sophisticated. I sipped the nightcap from my coffee cup. Eartha Kitt's throaty voice filled the softly shadowed basement room.

"I want to see my old home and friends in Amsterdam," I whispered.

"I'll take you there," he said and pulled me close.

"*Even the Dutch in Old Amsterdam do it . . .*" The lyrics drifted through the air and into our young, receptive ears and hearts.

"*Let's do it—let's fall in love.*"

I lost my virginity in the backseat of Pat's cream-and-green-colored Ford Custom. Shortly after I turned twenty, we were married. Our first child, a little girl whom we named Laura, after my sister, was born on Australia Day a year later. We were young and in love and told each other we were "meant for success."

At that time, many Australian companies desiring to strengthen and stimulate connections with England and other countries in the Western world paid for valued employees and sometimes their families to visit and study abroad, usually in return for a lengthy employment contract. When *The Advertiser* decided it would benefit the newspaper for its editorial cartoonist to meet with editors, journalists, and other cartoonists of the foreign press, we packed up our six-month-old baby daughter and flew off on a four-month journey around the world.

Pat did indeed visit Fleet Street, the center of the national press. Introductions from *The Advertiser* in hand, we were welcomed by editors of every major newspaper where our feet touched the ground. We roamed London. We found his ancestors in the graves of family churchyards in Scotland.

But the highlight for me was our visit to my old home and friends in Amsterdam and getting to introduce my Aussie baby daughter to family in Rotterdam. My slightly older cousins Netty and Loura, with whom I'd played constantly as a little girl, had their own children by this point as well and were thrilled to introduce them to their new Aussie cousin. My aunts and uncles took turns holding Laura and said as one, "Oh, she looks so Dutch. Look at her. She is a real Dutch girl."

It made me laugh, having heard the same comments on the other side of the world, where Pat's relatives claimed, "Oh, she's an Aussie. Look at her. She is our Aussie girl."

Yes, I thought with satisfaction. *She's "the right mix," as my American friends once said—a Dutch-Aussie!*

Laura thrived with all the love and attention with which she was lavished each day, and I felt my two worlds come together.

My uncle, one of the artists in Rotterdam, asked Pat about his art while showing him his own paintings. They discussed brush strokes, oil versus water paints, and the works of Rembrandt and Van Gogh. Pat praised the talent of my uncle, who in turn spoke up and said, "Well, frankly, I wasn't happy about Henny marrying an Australian at first. I thought she should have married a nice Dutch boy. They make good husbands. But you are okay. I like you. Welcome to the family."

He and the rest of the family all wanted to keep us in Holland. We left with the promise that we would one day return and visit again.

Then we were off to Paris, where we ate baguettes and cheese on a bench in the park and I honored my grandmother, who had encouraged the French in me. We saw New York and Los Angeles, fell in love with San Francisco. We told each other we would live there one day.

Our baby girl turned out to be a first-class world traveler, not to mention a magnet for all the help and care we needed along the way.

As it had when we'd attended the Journalists' Ball as the Mississippi steamboat gambler and his sexy moll, life felt magical. We were living our fairy-tale fantasy.

Chapter 34
A Married Woman
Adelaide, South Australia, 1963

"Well, I guess we traded in our dreams for marriage, didn't we?" Dot was the first to raise the issue.

She, Jane, and I had managed to schedule a mini reunion of sorts, except that we had evolved from milkshakes at the milk bar to coffees at the popular new Italian espresso bar on Rundle Street. It had been at least five years since we'd all been married. I had been back from the whirlwind round-the-world tour for almost four.

"Do you regret that you didn't become a stewardess and spend a few years flying around the world before marrying Brian?" Jane asked her.

"Just that I never got off the ground—that I had to make a choice, marriage or career," Dot said. "Airlines didn't want a married woman. Don't know that Brian would have waited." Now twenty-four years old, with one toddler and another baby on the way, she shrugged. "I try not to think about it. Right now, I'm thrilled to have a new washing machine for all the diapers I'll be washing. I figure we'll travel when the kids are older."

"I think it's unjust that you had to give up your dream to be a stewardess just because you married," I said. "Pilots don't have to give up their jobs when they marry."

"Women can't even be commercial pilots, married or not." Dot scowled.

"I know all that, but I enjoy being married," Jane said, "and the twins keep me from thinking too much."

"Do you ever regret not going to Italy to study singing?" I asked her.

She smiled and said softly, "Not really. I sing in the church choir, so I still use my voice. How about you? Do you ever miss being at the newspaper?"

"Oh yes, I miss the hustle and bustle," I said without hesitation. "The daily thrill of being in the middle of the news stories."

"And do you swim anymore?" Dot asked me.

"A little. I take the kids to the pool whenever I can. I've been teaching them to swim. I enjoy that. My parents keep reminding me how lucky I am: a successful husband, a beautiful home, and two healthy, delightful children—a girl and a boy, no less. I am a huge success. Even a naturalized Australian citizen now."

"Sounds like my parents," Jane said, and Dot nodded.

"Did you know that Helen moved to New York for her modeling career?" Dot volunteered.

"Good on her for following her dreams," I said. "You heard from her?"

"Just a postcard a year or so ago."

The three of us sat in silence for a while.

"I wouldn't give up being a mother for anything in the world, and I love my husband, but if I have to polish that black-and-white kitchen floor to a pristine sheen one more time, I'm going to puke all over it," I piped up, "and I really can't get excited over the new refrigerator."

We laughed.

"At least we are not old maids!" Dot chuckled.

It was good to reconnect and see her humor surface again.

"Is that how we are going to raise our daughters?" I asked. "When mine was born, my old boss at *The Advertiser* sent me a note congratulating us. It was nice, but he wrote that she would 'no doubt' apply for my old job one day. Is there really 'no doubt' that our daughters will always be assigned jobs that serve the men in charge? What if she wants to be a journalist, or maybe the editor or the chief of staff of a newsroom? Or a political cartoonist like her father?"

"You think women should have the same opportunities as men," Jane said with a wry smile.

"I want to make a difference in the world, the way my mother did when she joined the Resistance and risked everything to stand up to the Nazis in Amsterdam," I said firmly.

"No, no, you are a married woman in Australia." Dot wagged a finger at me. "Remember, we clean, we cook, we take care of the kids and serve our husbands with a smile. That's our role!"

As if rehearsed, the three of us burst into hysterical guffaws of laughter that felt like a release from pretending that in marriage, we had found ourselves living happily ever after.

"My mother was a married woman at that time," I reminded them.

"But your father was away in a POW camp, right? It was wartime. People were being killed." Jane's warm voice filled the space between us with her thoughtful reflection.

Her words would linger in my mind long after we had parted and I had made my way to the corner of the street to wait for the bus that would take me home.

We promised to meet again soon, but in the ensuing years, our encounters became less frequent. Jane moved to a country town in Victoria; Dot mentioned marital troubles she couldn't discuss; Pat and I were considering a possible move to the US for his career.

Gradually, we lost touch—but I never forgot our conversations. Knowing that other women felt the way I did made me feel less alone and helped me deal with the sense of injustice I had been feeling at Australia's insistence that a woman's place was in the home—an attitude that prevented many married women from pursuing valuable careers.

My conversation with my married women friends stayed with me as I boarded the bus to return to the three-bedroom suburban home Pat and I had bought at the urging of his parents shortly after the birth of our second child, Grant. An adorable, blue-eyed, blond little boy, Grant was just two years younger than his inquisitive older sister, who delighted me each night with her insistent demands that I tell her more stories.

"Tell me another one, Mummy," she'd urge.

"Oh, honey, I have read you all the stories," I'd say.

"Just make one up," she would say, curling up against me. "I like your made-up stories best."

She would get another story, of course, and for a precious moment, my mind would feel fully engaged and my imagination valued.

What will the world look like by the time she becomes a young woman? I would wonder.

The bus came to an abrupt stop, its sudden jolt halting my inner reverie. We had arrived at my destination. I walked the three blocks past the manicured lawns of the pristine housing development to our look-alike home, where my mother had been taking care of the children for the day.

It seemed unusually quiet when I opened the front door. My mom looked up from the chair in which she had been reclining and put down her book.

I glanced at the title. "Another biography? Helen Keller? And in English? You are just becoming too smart, Mum."

"What do you mean?" She laughed. "I was always smart. Both your beautiful daughter and handsome son are still down for their nap. They are the best children ever."

My mother's beauty struck me in that moment, as it often did others. Despite the traumas she'd faced in WWII Amsterdam—death, betrayal, starvation—and the challenges she'd experienced starting a new life in Australia far away from the support of her own family, culture, and language, including that year in the flyblown mallee scrub desert without electricity or running water, she had maintained her trim, athletic figure, and her face glowed with health and a joy for life.

"How was your reunion?" she asked.

"It was good, but sort of sad also," I admitted. "It's as if we have all become what we were told to be. We have lost our uniqueness. We are nice housewives and good mothers. Acceptable, comfortable."

My mother did not respond.

"I miss the dreams that made us interesting. It's as if we lose our color, our individuality, as women when we marry. We, I don't know, become black-and-white carbon copies of every other housewife, stamped with approval." I looked at my mother, wanting a response. "We were going to sing and fly and write. I thought I was going to make a difference in the world, like you did when you decided to join the Resistance. Now I iron, cook, and clean."

"But, Henny, that was survival." My mother looked shocked. "It was about life and death. We had to fight. We were standing up against evil! It's peacetime now. You should be grateful. You can raise your children in a beautiful home without being afraid. That's what we fought for."

"That's what my friend Jane said, and I understand," I said. "But why is it that women are always being told where they belong? We don't belong in the newsroom, or on the flight deck. And it gets worse when we marry. Suddenly, we belong only in the home. It's a waste of women's minds and talents, Mum."

My mother frowned. "You sound just like my mother."

She did not make it sound like a compliment.

My grandfather, who had died when my mother was only nineteen, had been a dreamer, lost in the beauty of his own architectural designs. My grandmother had run their huge household of seven sons and three daughters like a modern CEO. She would have made an excellent business manager.

"She often told my sisters and me that women should be running the world," my mother said.

We both laughed.

"Well, we know that men won't allow that to happen—especially Australian men," I quipped, which made my mother frown again.

At that moment, both my husband and father drove up in their respective cars. They were standing outside, seemingly deep in conversation, when I opened the front door to greet them both.

My dad gave me a big hug and, stepping inside, immediately asked, "Hey, where are your children? The house is way too quiet."

"We thought we'd go pick up some beer and fish and chips for dinner," Pat said, following him in.

"They're napping," my mother said, "but it's probably time for Laura to wake up."

"Oh, I am sure she is awake," my dad said in a voice loud enough for Laura to hear as he walked into the children's bedroom, where he lifted his granddaughter out of her "big girl" bed and hugged her close. "You can come with us men," he said, setting her down but holding on to her hand. She giggled as the three of them walked out of the house.

I snuggled my two-year-old son, my cheek against his, while I put him in his chair. Nothing in my life felt quite as miraculous as my children did.

"Henny." My mom looked at me. "You have so much to be grateful for. Don't tempt fate."

I did not respond, and she went about mixing a salad and setting the table with plates and cutlery while I fed my son, who enjoyed the attention both his grandmother and I settled on him.

The truth was that I did feel grateful, but I also felt a sense of injustice that I could not let go of. Something in me had been shaken when it was naturally assumed I would stay at home when I was married at age twenty. I had always admired the strong independence my mother had showcased when my dad was absent during the war years. Why were women only seen as capable of heroics when they were alone, when the men were away at war or dead? What was it about being a married woman that made me feel as if my brain had been scooped out?

Soon the men returned with our dinner, and the mouthwatering smell of hot, beer-battered chunks of fish and fried chips chased away all troubling thoughts.

"Well, we certainly have enough food," my mother said in her best English, and I saw the look of contentment on her face as she handed my son a piece of fried potato.

"And plenty of cold beer," Pat added with a laugh. "The boss made sure of that." He poured me a glass with lots of foam, the way I liked it.

I watched the three generations around my kitchen table and saw the calm joy, the promised peace and abundance of the Australian life for which my parents had left everything familiar behind all those many years ago. For a moment, a deep feeling of admiration and gratitude for their courage washed over me.

When my parents left, Pat turned, put his arm around me, and said, "I really like your old man. I told him I want to move to the US because there's more freedom of expression for political cartoonists in American newspapers, and that they should come, too."

"We still have a year to go on your contract," I said softly.

"That's not long," he said. "We need to get ready."

I felt a pang of apprehension. I had been excited about our plans to move to the States, but now I wondered, *Ready for what?*

Chapter 35
Destination USA
Adelaide, South Australia, 1964

Our bags are packed. All belongings have been shipped to America. In less than a week, my two children, their father, and I will board an Ansett plane from Adelaide to Sydney. A Qantas jet will take us to San Francisco, where we will see my parents and sister, who sailed ahead of us. Our final destination will be Denver, Colorado, a new place to call home.

We planned to settle in San Francisco, but capricious destiny threw her dice and changed our path. How could the steamboat gambler and his moll resist the challenge when we heard that the *Denver Post*, a major US newspaper, was losing its respected editorial cartoonist, Paul Conrad, to a move to Los Angeles and was therefore looking for a new political cartoonist? Of course, it had to be my husband.

"It's destiny," we said.

But tonight, one last time, I walk alone along the beach where I have swum a thousand swims. It is a clear winter's night. I carry my shoes and go barefoot at the water's edge. The surf communicates its South Australian July winter chill to my feet. The Southern Cross sparkles brightly above my head. Its stars pull me back to the first time I ever saw the constellation that would continue to mesmerize me in the years I grew from Dutch girl to Aussie woman.

For a moment, I am again the thirteen-year-old Dutch migrant girl just off the boat. I am walking with my father in the deep darkness of the empty scrub desert, my hand in his. We look up at the alien sky together. He points to two stars and then, there just beyond—"look carefully now, it is the Southern Cross." A beacon of light shines in the darkness.

Gratitude, that emotion my mother has taught me to feel even in the most desperate times, surges through my body. I offer a silent prayer of thanks to this ancient land and the people who welcomed and supported us. They have shaped me into the woman I have become.

The little child in me will always think of Amsterdam as home, but the teenager will forever claim Australia as her own. She will treasure memories of Aussie sportsmanship and camaraderie, remember the sun and the beaches, the hours spent in amniotic waters, and never forget the flyblown initiation of the land of "grubs and water soakage." And yes, she will "bloody well have two queens."

The evening dark closes around me. A powerful wave pounds into my legs, causing me to stumble and reminding me that I have wandered up to my knees into this beloved sea that has always supported my will and strength.

Toes curled in the cold, wet sand, I direct my legs toward the shore and take a deep inhale of the salty ocean air. I look up at the Southern Cross one last time.

I have belonged here, but now I am leaving the Aussie womb. Hit by unexpected fear and grief, I hear my mother's words: "Intentions are like prayers." But what is my intention for our life in the US?

I fear I am not the woman I intended to be. I have not helped others the way my mother once did in WWII or gained the respect she earned through her heroic efforts.

One last time, Australia, this timeless land—or maybe it's the ocean, or perhaps it's the Southern Cross, or God, or the Universe, or a voice in my own head—speaks to me, and the words ring out loud and clear: "You have not yet become the woman you will be. There is more to be discovered. Do not be afraid."

I allow the tears to stream down my face. And I slowly begin to walk home, where my husband and children await me.

Just over two years from now, on the other side of the world in Denver, Colorado, my husband will win the prestigious Pulitzer Prize for his biting political cartoons. I will give birth to our third child, a beautiful little girl named Susanne. The first American in our family, she will choose to be born on George Washington's birthday. I will participate in a communal childcare group in an RV on the Denver extension campus of the University of Colorado, where young mothers exchange childcare hours and juggle course studies in pursuit of the college degrees that we hope will lead to our future careers.

I will read Simone de Beauvoir and Gloria Steinem, meet Betty Friedan, study Dr. Carl Jung, obtain master's degrees in theology and counseling psychology, and search for the Feminine Face of God. I will help other women discover the woman they intend to be. There will be geographical moves and emotional detours and challenges. I will divorce, have other relationships, and ultimately find deep joy in a later marriage. I will keep swimming, and it will be a long, rich life.

But that is the American part of my story.

Acknowledgments

This book would not have been completed without the help and encouragement of my amazing global community of friends, family, former students and clients, readers, and swimmers.

When you are writing a memoir about a stage of life that happened decades ago, it helps if you can revisit the places where it all happened and reconnect with the people who knew you way back then. A huge thanks goes to my Aussie friends and family for your generosity in schlepping me around to familiar spots while encouraging me to write my story. To Maryanne Mooney, I love you for insisting you drive me back to revisit Ki Ki, so I could hug the gum trees and stand once again on the old tennis courts. Thank you for asking all the right questions that made me recollect crucial details about life in the railway cottages, my first home in Australia, as we walked on the grounds next to the tracks where they once stood. To Mike and Helen Burleigh, I owe you a deep gratitude for the drive from Sydney to Bathurst so I could reexperience and write about the awe I felt when I first saw the magnificent beauty of the Blue Mountains as a young Dutch girl. Thank you for graciously hosting my husband and me in your vineyard home in Bathurst and giving me the opportunity to visit the historic site of the old Bathurst migrant reception center. It felt magical and added important details. And, dear old friend Jim Smith, my deepest gratitude for helping me relocate familiar sites in Rundle and Hindley streets, visit the beach where once stood the old Henley Beach pool, and reconnecting me with Pauline. Thank you, Pauline, for your generous response to our spur of the moment visit and for your helpful reflections on the old newsroom and its reporters. Such a gift.

My gratitude to the amazing Aussie swimmers, Olympians in every way. Dale Krieg (Knappstein) and Margaret Gibson (Messenger), how lovely to reconnect by mail and phone. Thank you for sharing and rekindling memories, for reading early chapter notes and reminding me of details I overlooked. And a big thank you to Jon Henricks for your kind praise of my Amsterdam memoir and your encouragement to keep on writing even as our memories "mature."

To Roger Edmonds of the Henley and Grange Historical Society in South Australia for our video interview. It brought back vivid memories of swimming laps in the old Henley Pool, a small part of which is now enshrined in the cover image of my book.

And to my Australian friend and Santa Barbara neighbor, Ross Ray, a dedicated Rotarian, who passed away while I was writing this book—your grace and humor in helping me remember and clarify Aussie terms and expressions live on in my heart and in my story.

To the hardworking team and author sisterhood of She Writes Press which also published my first memoir, *When a Toy Dog Became a Wolf and the Moon Broke Curfew*, my deep appreciation for helping me bring forth this sequel. Brooke Warner, thank you for upholding your standards of excellence in publishing and for your untiring support and guidance. Krissa Lagos, I am indebted to you not only for your pertinent questions when editing my manuscript, but also for challenging my propensity for invisibility. Lauren Wise and Shannon

Green, my gratitude for your availability and willingness to answer questions, respond to emails with suggestions, repeat timelines, and offer reassurances. And, of course, a shout out to Julie Metz and her cover design team.

For many years I've been fortunate to attend the annual Santa Barbara Writers Conference where inspiring workshops and presenters have provided a safe place to explore, write, and share story ideas and proposals. I especially want to thank Grace Rachow for her untiring support of us scribblers, and memoir teachers Diana Raab and Catherine Jones for their valuable expertise and motivating insights.

A big gratitude to my friend for life, Ann Shaw, who took care of my cats when I was away and left food at the door when I was sick, while she created the photos, images, and website for my first memoir. Thank you for helping me with cover images and title suggestions as I explored publishing options for this sequel, and for your continual creative support. And to my circle of longtime women friends Mary Leibman, Kate Smith-Hanssen, Karen Friess-Perrino, and Serena Carroll, who kept lovingly bugging me for the Australian sequel to my first memoir. Thanks for giving me that necessary playful push as I procrastinated and hesitated.

My inspiring colleagues, scholars who have written and published numerous books, Christine Downing, Maureen Murdock, and Dennis Slattery, thank you for your praise of my Amsterdam memoir and encouragement to write its Australian sequel. You gave me the necessary confidence.

A huge loving Thank You to Joris Vos, fellow "Netherlander" and former Dutch ambassador to Australia and the US, for gifting me with your spontaneous translation of my memoir *When a Toy Dog Became a Wolf and the Moon Broke Curfew* into Dutch, affirming the global history behind my stories of the war and immigration—and your continuing support of my writing voice.

My sister, Laura, of course. Thank you, Sis, for emboldening me to write and publish our family immigration story, when I had my doubts.

I thank my three adult children, who have always shown their interest in our family stories and encouraged my writing. I am a lucky mom. And my husband Harlan Green who not only encourages and supports my writing, but who swims with me and brings me morning coffee with a smile and words of love.

This book could not have been written without all of you and many others, who are not mentioned here because that would take a whole other book.

About the Author

photo credit: Ann MacNair Shaw

Hendrika de Vries is a retired family therapist, a teacher, and a writer. Her life experiences with oppression and resistance in Nazi-occupied Amsterdam; migration, competitive swimming, and misogyny in 1950s Australia; and feminism in the US infuse her writing with historical depth and personal perspective on challenges facing women and anyone deemed inferior. She is the author of *When a Toy Dog Became a Wolf and the Moon Broke Curfew,* an award-winning memoir of her WWII childhood. A mother, grandmother, and great-grandmother, she lives with her husband, Harlan, on the Santa Barbara Riviera, California.

Looking for your next great read?

We can help!

Visit www.shewritespress.com/next-read
or scan the QR code below for a list
of our recommended titles.

She Writes Press is an award-winning
independent publishing company founded to
serve women writers everywhere.